HIS GIFT *My Story*

KIM COLLINGSWORTH

with
BECKY KEEP

P&KC
MUSIC

HIS GIFT ... MY STORY

First Edition

Cover photography and design services by Courtney Collingsworth Metz
All photography courtesy of the author

Library of Congress Cataloging-in-Publication Data has been applied for.

ISBN 978-1-948362-49-8

Published by Whispering Pines Publishers, Shoals, Indiana.

Printed in the United States of America.

CONTENTS

Acknowledgments 5

Introduction 9

1   The Gift 13

2   The Awakening of the Gift 19

3   It's A Calling, Not a Career 35

4   How We Met 53

5   Take a Step of Faith 69

6   Tuesday Evening Prayers 87

7   How Did We Do That? 105

8   Sitting at the End of the Table 123

9   When God Opens the Door 141

10   Tales You Won't Hear from the Stage 161

11   Memorable People, Memorable Times 175

12   Joy in a Canceled World 191

Q & A with Kim 209

ACKNOWLEDGMENTS

To my parents, James and Carolyn Keaton, who loved and protected me as a child, while still allowing me to blossom and grow. I am indebted to you. Thank you for introducing me to Jesus. I was taught the importance of loving and serving him by watching your daily example. Your deep faith and unwavering commitment to God and each other still inspires me greatly. You are simply the best, and I love you both deeply.

To Becky Keep, my forever sister and friend. Did we ever dream all those years ago, when we were two little girls—sisters sharing a room, our clothes, and life in a big family—that we would embark upon such a journey together? Your ability to craft words into a beautiful story is admirable but certainly not surprising. Thinking back, you always did like a good storyline as a child. I have enjoyed walking memory lane with you. I will look back with fondness on our time spent together in preparation for this book. Reminiscing of times past and reveling in the goodness and providence of God with you has been good for my heart. Thanks for being willing to share this journey in such an intricate way. I can't think of anyone else who could know my story any better from the very beginning than you. I love you, sis!

To William, Michael, and Sharlenae. I have often thanked God for you. When my children were small I began praying for their future spouses. Though I didn't know it would be you, I specifically prayed that God would give you a deep, unwavering love for him. He has answered my prayers in the three of you. We are beyond blessed to have you as part of our family. My love for each of you runs deep, and I feel as if you are my own. Thank you for your tireless efforts for this ministry. It's unconventional, and how it all works I will never understand, but your incredible support is nothing short of impressive. I love each of you!

To Emma, Winston, Noah, Theo, and Wellington, my precious grandchildren! I had no idea my heart could hold so much love until you began to arrive on the scene. You light up my life, and I love you so very much! I pray often for each of you. My prayer is that you will love and serve Jesus. Always remember, the One who has carried your Nana and Papa through every hard place will never let you down.

To Brooklyn, Courtney, Phillip, and Olivia. You are gifts to me in more ways than I could ever express. Your joyful willingness to happily support and share, from the time you were small, in the calling that God placed upon your dad's life, has been a blessing to behold. It wasn't always easy, but your eagerness to join in and become such a vital part has made the journey so sweet.

Thank you for your patience with me on the crazy journey of home-schooling. You were troopers…every single one of you! You have now transitioned from being my sweet little babies to beautiful adults whom I admire and respect greatly. You have become some of my closest and dearest friends. No doubt, as you read this book, many memories will come flooding back. Over the years, we've laughed a lot together, had fun together, prayed together, and watched God's will for our lives and family unfold right before our eyes. Perhaps my greatest gift of all is the love you have for one another and for our Savior. Nothing could make my heart happier. I love you endlessly!

To Phil Collingsworth, my amazing husband and the love of my life, you are in a league all your own. Outside of my Lord and Savior, Jesus Christ, you are the best thing that has ever happened to me! You know me *best*, yet love me *most*. Your ability to see beyond the mundane never ceases to impress me. Thinking "outside the box" is an everyday occurrence for you that used to utterly terrify me, but is now something

I've come to appreciate and cherish about you. Thank you for seeing in me what I never could have seen in myself. You pulled me from behind the curtain (my comfort zone) and into the action because you believed in me. We are definitely better together, and I wouldn't want it any other way. I will always love you!

INTRODUCTION

Sunday, March 15, 2020, dawned crisp and bright. "Black Pearl," as our Prevost H3-45 tour bus is affectionately named, carried us across the heartland of the nation for the twenty-hour trip home to Mt. Orab, Ohio. We stood before an audience in Keene, Texas, the previous night, our third concert of the weekend. It seemed like any other concert weekend of the past twenty years. The Collingsworth Family had traversed the highways of the continental United States and Canada many times. But today, everything was changing.

Phil's cell phone buzzed continuously as we traveled toward home. Each text, email, or voicemail signaled another concert postponement or cancellation. Alarm, uncertainty, and fear were almost palpable in the atmosphere around us.

The nation was gripped with fear of the largely unknown coronavirus, COVID-19. Media outlets were spewing frightening statistics about hospitalizations, ventilator shortages, and ever-soaring death rates. Government officials were establishing task forces, and public health officials were making dire predictions.

As we pulled into the P&KC Music warehouse that evening, the conversations were subdued, contemplative, and questioning, as each individual family unit gathered their belongings and transferred them to their vehicles. After slipping off into the night to their respective homes, quiet settled over The Collingsworth Family homeplace. Phil and I set our luggage down in our bedroom and wished Olivia a good night. We brewed fresh coffee and sat down together, exchanging questioning looks and wondering aloud, *"What is happening!?"* In just one day, our world had come to a sudden standstill, as had the worlds of so many others, including our fellow artists and music industry colleagues.

We sat at the kitchen counter, notebooks in hand, and began discussing the realities of our business operations—payroll, health insurance, ongoing expenses, reserves, balances on hand, income/loss, etc. When the sky turned pink over the tree line the next morning, we were still there—exploring scenarios, discussing the possible length of the quarantine, wondering what our future might hold, calling on our heavenly Father. We begged for his direction and guidance through this new, unknown world.

As the days turned into weeks and the weeks into months, we began to grasp, in a very personal way, the reassuring and unwavering truth that, "Every morning his mercies are new!" I settled into a new routine, rising in the morning and moving, *first*, toward our faithful Keurig. After "pouring" a rich, fragrant cup of coffee, I'd settle into my favorite place in "The Haven." There, with my Bible, journal, and some rich reading materials I'd gain insight and strength from their only true Source.

Somewhere, in the early weeks of our mandatory shutdown in Ohio, I began to sense that perhaps this was God's timing to put my story on paper. Although I had been asked many times to write our story, I had never seriously considered it until now. My schedule would have never allowed for it anyway. One Sunday afternoon, with both immediate and some extended family gathered for a delicious Sunday dinner, talk suddenly turned toward the potential of writing this book. It seemed *too* sudden at first. *Am I prepared?* I wondered. But as the conversation continued, it dawned upon me that God had been preparing me for this moment for more than twenty-five years. I thought about the stacks of journals I'd filled since my childhood, and I remembered the strong prompting I'd felt all those years ago, to record my thoughts and the events of my life. The journals were discussed around the table, and I was challenged to organize them—to categorize, to place them in order of sequence, to begin the process of gleaning material for the writing of my first book.

Before the day was over, a sketch of these chapters had been scribbled down. And by the time the sun rose the next morning, the marathon was on! This was COVID. This was quarantine. This was unplanned time off which may never come my way again. Why not take full advantage of this unforeseen moment!?

Pre-COVID, I had asked the Lord, many times, for a short break; for a rest from the constant demands of concert ministry—new record production, preparing public music presentations, maintaining a demanding schedule with twelve people and all their belongings, and juggling a hundred logistical challenges. The Lord gently reminded me that while this was an unconventional method of answering my request, he had indeed provided what I desperately needed. I felt myself begin to relax, knowing he definitely had it all under control. The fact that I was actually getting to sleep in my own bed, at home, for more nights in a row than I had in thirty-eight years, almost seemed too good to be true! And now I had time to write.

I jumped into the process of reading and organizing twenty-five years of journal entries. I read with amazement the recorded events and reflections I'd forgotten long ago. I chose a writer, and started interviews with her immediately. My sister, Becky Keep and I spent countless hours together. We laughed and cried over the amazing, sometimes terrifying, and often miraculous things God had done. Walking memory lane has been a really good exercise!

Phil has jumped into this process too. He has laughed and cried with me as we've edited these chapters. He's collected, captioned, and numbered photo images from both our lives. He's jumped into interview sessions with Becky and me, spending hours with us, and pulling intricate, forgotten details out of thin air. Together, we've marveled at the paths God has taken us down. Writing has provided a fresh vantage point for us—a vantage point of more than five decades of life, three decades of marriage, and two decades of ministry. As we've looked back over our path and traced the hand of God, we stand amazed.

As I read my journals and recalled the highlights, the chapters began to fall into place. It's been challenging to know exactly which incidents to include and which to leave for another day. The volume of events was overwhelming. After months of writing, interviews, corrections, advice, and collaboration; after all the digging through old photo albums, Facebook pages, and external hard drives; after countless hours of reading, re-reading, consultations, and gallons of delicious coffee...*His Gift, My Story* is a reality.

My prayer is that through the stories and insights shared in these pages, your faith will increase. I pray that in *your* heart will arise a deeper love, a greater appreciation, and a more profound awe for God—our Father and the Creator of the universe—who from the beginning of time, has been intricately involved in the affairs of men. This God converges on our life's pathway at the most unexpected moments, to show with unparalleled splendor, his presence and fatherly care. I am eternally grateful!

I love you all,
Kim

———

1

THE GIFT

Jesus said, "Let the little children come to me, and do not hinder them,
for the kingdom of heaven belongs to such as these."
—Matthew 19:14

I exited the double glass doors of the church in a hurry and ran down the three stairs to the sidewalk below. I made a left turn, and as fast as my 3-year-old legs would carry me, raced down the sidewalk, across the gravel drive, and up the front porch stairs of the parsonage where our family lived. I barely slowed as I opened the screen door, scurried through a small kitchen and dining room, entered the living room, and made my way to a stairwell in the corner. I dashed up those stairs—all fourteen of them—without stopping to catch my breath. I was on a mission.

I was born December 6, 1968, the fifth of nine children. I arrived just after my parents' sixth wedding anniversary, and entered a family that was already teeming with little people. My parents, feeling a bit overwhelmed with the responsibilities of so many children, had decided I would be their last. My mother had surgery when I was three days old to ensure there would be no more babies. I can't imagine her shock when she discovered a mere fifteen months later there would be yet another

Keaton baby coming—oops! And then there were three more after my sister Becky, which made us a family of eleven.

My dad was a pastor and evangelist. My first memories are of the white country parsonage we lived in as a family in New Albany, Indiana, where my dad pastored the Clear Fork Wesleyan Church. The six years we spent there were formative to me in so many ways.

The church and parsonage were located on a rural road that wound through beautiful countryside. It was quiet and peaceful. We were surrounded by pastureland and woods. There was a creek that ran just behind our property where we played for hours on summer days. I loved catching the brown crawdads that lived in the muddy water, but not so much when they resisted and gave my finger a pinch. On late summer evenings, my older siblings would sometimes take us all across the road and up a steep hill where we played "Ghost in the graveyard." Lying our little bodies down in front of old tombstones and then pretending to rise from the dead was wonderfully fun and left us all delightfully scared and running down the hill toward home! We had no television, and spent a lot of time creating our own entertainment. Mom always took us to the library on Saturday where, when I was a bit older, I checked out the "Little House on the Prairie" books and spent many happy evenings curled up in a corner reading about the adventures of Laura and Mary.

I recall the day we children were excited about the new table that was carried into our house and situated in the dining room. This was no ordinary table. Dad had this table handcrafted to meet the demands of our growing family. Even as a little girl, I felt like we had arrived. Our family had a table that was made especially for us! Dad emphasized that this table had to be sturdy—sturdy enough to withstand nine rowdy kids and thousands of family dinners. The carpenter bolted and double bolted the top to the frame and legs of the table. He then made two beautiful benches to accommodate all of us.

That table facilitated countless happy times for the rest of our growing up years. We all had our assigned seats. The boys sat to dad's right, oldest to youngest along those long benches. And we girls were seated to his left, oldest to youngest. Although there were so many of us, and I'm sure things were chaotic at times, mealtimes were organized, and we were taught to be mannerly and to conduct ourselves properly at the table.

I loved sitting quietly at that table late into the evening after a revival service as mom and dad lingered, chatting with the visiting evangelists. I loved the stories of their many travels and the interesting people they had encountered along the way. There was one particular missionary evangelist who came several times and who was a bit unconventional. As soon as he arrived, he would climb a tree in our yard and mount his shortwave radio antenna. We children could hardly wait for dinner around the table with George Hawthorne. Not only was he funny and entertaining, but he always placed a pack of chewing gum at each of our plates. We loved it! We rarely had this kind of treat. Dad and mom also brought many desperate people into our home and fed them around that same table, while sharing the Gospel with them.

Mostly, our lives revolved around the church. There was Wednesday night prayer meeting, Saturday night prayer meeting, Sunday morning worship, and the Sunday evening evangelistic service. And the people who made up the church were a colorful array of personalities, vocations, and backgrounds.

There was the Barger family who lived on a farm not far from the church. Melvin Barger was a plumber by day, but operated a busy farm on the side. Each week they delivered several gallons of fresh cow's milk to the parsonage. Stella Barger was a sweet, soft-spoken lady who wore her hair in two braids wrapped around the top of her head. She was the one who prayed with me the night I was saved. I can still remember her voice, and the scent of woodsmoke, as she laid her soft hand on my back, and with tears, prayed for my salvation.

There was the church "candy man" who had all kinds of delightful treats in the trunk of his car. All the children in the church followed him there after the service to see what he had to offer. I was always a tad disappointed when, instead of candy, he offered us granola. We Keaton kids didn't have access to many sweets or candy back in the day, so this was always exciting for us.

There was a lady named Barbara who had several children, and was known to be a prayer warrior. I revered her and knew that she walked with Jesus. Our song leader, Gene Voyles, put much thought and prayer into his preparation for Sunday morning worship, and always sang a special song just before the sermon.

I remember the testimonies on Wednesday nights, and even as a small child, I was aware of God's presence as people stood and gave Him praise for how He was at work in their lives; how He had answered their prayers, supplied their needs, strengthened them in weakness, and comforted them in moments of distress.

Although our family was large and my mom was busy, she served as church pianist. She was accomplished and had her own style. Mom was happy-go-lucky and would often play funny songs for us children at home on our old upright while we danced around the coffee table.

I can't imagine what it must have been like for her, trying to get us all ready and out the door for church on time. Dad was usually at the church early, so this task was left up to mom. We all knew exactly what was expected of us in church. We sat on the second row, right side, lined up beside our mother. The older kids sometimes were able to move to the third row, and occasionally we were allowed to sit in front of mom on the first row.

Dad utilized us in the ministry from the time we were very young. My very first act of church ministry was to fold the bulletins on Sunday morning before service. Dad carefully showed us how to do it, emphasizing folding and making a sharp crease, and how to keep the edges together and straight. I took this job very seriously. It was important and I wanted to get it right.

Sometimes church seemed long—especially since we didn't have the luxury of children's church to entertain us back then. And mom had her hands full just hauling all of us and herself to the church. She usually didn't pack much in the way of toys, snacks, or books. We sat quietly—or sometimes *not* so quietly—for the duration. My sister Becky and I were thrilled when we could find a pen and circle each individual word in the Sunday school paper. You could burn up quite a bit of the Sunday morning sermon doing this.

Our services were punctuated by God's presence, and even as a small child I experienced conviction and the Holy Spirit tugging at my heart. He was drawing me as a little girl, and there were many times when dad would give an invitation, and my siblings and I would go forward and seek the Lord. Dad and mom always encouraged us, and it was at that altar that I gave my heart to Jesus.

One particular night, I remember sitting on the front row all the way in on the aisle seat. It was a typical Sunday evening. We had enjoyed an energetic song service, announcements, offering, and prayer. Dad was now preaching, and I was busy with something in my lap. Dad was a very interesting preacher, and had a way of capturing the attention of even the very young. He always told colorful illustrations, and knew just when to insert a bit of humor into the sermon. It wasn't any of these, however, that caused me to stop and listen on this night. My three-year-old mind was suddenly captivated by the Bible story dad was telling. It was about a king in the Bible who asked God for a gift. He asked for wisdom. Dad went on to tell how King Solomon was the wisest man who ever lived. I remember thinking that there had been a "wisest man," but not a "wisest woman."

Daddy's words, "Solomon asked for a gift, and God graciously granted it," deeply penetrated my childish heart and mind. I don't remember another word that was spoken. I do remember thinking to myself, "*I am going to ask God for a gift—as soon as I get home tonight, I am going to ask him!*"

After tearing up that flight of stairs, I ran into the large bedroom that I shared with my younger sister. I pulled out the drawer that held my pajamas. I quickly changed out of my church dress, and knelt at the end of my bed. I squeezed my eyes shut and prayed with all the faith and sincerity that a three-year-old could possess. *"Jesus, will you please give me a gift, like the one you gave to that king my daddy was preaching about tonight?"* And to make sure Jesus knew just how badly I wanted that gift, I did what I always did when I prayed. I held up both hands and punctuated the raising of each finger with the word, "Please!" until all ten fingers were outstretched. *"Please, Jesus, give me a gift!"*

I didn't tell mom when she tucked me in that evening about my prayer. I didn't tell anyone for more than a decade. I drifted off to sleep in expectant anticipation—thinking, *"I can't wait to see what I am when I wake up tomorrow morning!"* I just *knew* God had heard me and would grant my request. And although I felt sharply disappointed to find upon waking that I was no different than I had been the night before, I know now, that God had indeed heard the prayer of a sincere little girl. I didn't become the female version of Solomon, but years later I understood that God had graciously granted a gift. And somehow, I have always known that the *gift* He gave was connected to the *prayer* of a child. I believe He planted a seed that very night—something within that little girl who was me, which He would use for HIS glory and for His purpose in this world. It was His gift to give, and He shared it with me. How I thank Him!

2

THE AWAKENING OF THE GIFT

Do not neglect your gift, which was given you...
—I Timothy 4:14

Talent is cheap, dedication is expensive....it will cost you your life.
—Irving Stone

I clearly remember when I first became aware that I could play the piano.

My mother says I began climbing up onto the piano bench between ages three and four, and picking out tunes with one finger. But my first *memory* began at the supper table one evening after finishing our meal of meatloaf and mashed potatoes. I was just four years old. My older siblings were beginning to drift from the table, and my sister Sandy, five years older than me, went to the old upright piano situated just next to our dining room. I watched and listened closely as she played through her recital piece. I don't remember the song, but thought to myself, *I can play that!*

She finished playing, and I made my way to the piano to try my hand. I sat on the bench, my short legs dangling far from the pedals, but those notes and chords were ringing in my ears. I carefully found each one and played the piece through. Mom remembers coming into the room and asking me with incredulity, "How did you learn to play that!?" She tells me that I shrugged and said, "She played it, and I wanted to play it, too."

I fell in love with the piano that day, and according to my mother, clambering up onto the piano bench to play was the first thing I did every morning, and the last thing I did before going to bed at night. She recalls many times having to shoo me off the bench and up the stairs to my room at bedtime. She was a busy mommy of young children, and sometimes my clanging and banging was like fingernails on a chalkboard, but she intentionally allowed me to play, and even encouraged me to do so. I loved being in the beautiful Indiana outdoors with my siblings, but my days were always punctuated by forays into the house, where I'd jump up onto that piano bench and play away. The tunes and chord structures I heard on the radio, record player, or at church danced around in my head like colorful butterflies caught in a net and just had to find their way out and onto the keys!

When I was about six years of age, our family traveled to a church convention in Dayton, Ohio; a three-day event with several thousand attendees. Throughout the day there were worship services which highlighted inspiring messages and wonderful music. One afternoon, a man named Archie Coons played a piano solo for an offertory. I was mesmerized! He was accomplished and had a unique style, but when he played a scaled run right in the middle of his selection, I was *smitten. I have never heard anything so amazing or beautiful,* I thought. My parents bought the cassette tape of that service, and I listened to that piano solo at least fifty times. I would rewind the tape to hear that beautiful run over and over again, and I remember being so eager to share this with my two little friends at church. After service one evening, Annette and Rebecca followed me to our home next door. We gathered around a clunky old tape recorder, and with a dramatic, "You're gonna love this!" I queued it up and pushed "play." When my sweet friends didn't respond at all I was stupefied! *Perhaps they hadn't heard the run,* I thought, so I rewound the tape and tried again. They remained unimpressed, and I couldn't have been more disappointed.

The guest musicians whom we received at our church left an indelible impression on me as a young girl. I would get to church early to secure a seat on the front row, piano side. I watched amazed as Jan Lasalle played the prelude and offertories. I was so impressed when she crossed her right hand over her left to play the melody in the bass. I noticed every detail when Henry and Jan Miller sang, and took note of Jan's beautiful command of the piano.

My years of growing up in church shaped me musically. The wealth of knowledge I gained about the hymns, their chord structures, and lyrics, was permanently imprinted in my mind. When I learned how to read, I spent many church services reading through the hymnal, with a goal to learn every song in the book. I would slowly turn the pages, read the titles, and make a mental checklist. *I know this song, and this one. Don't know that one, know this one....* And on and on I would go. I childishly skipped over a few that looked too boring to learn. "The Macedonian Cry" was one I had no interest in. The lyric just didn't catch me as a little girl, though I'm sure it is a beautiful song.

I recall the first time my dad called upon me to play a piano solo in church. I was six. I played a simple version of "Fill My Cup, Lord," and a lady named Joyce Bunch played along on her bass guitar.

One Sunday morning, when I was eight, I stood in front of the mirror in my mother's room as she combed my hair. It was like every other Sunday morning—things were a bit hectic and we were hurrying to get to church on time. She said calmly, "Kimberly, mother is running late this morning, so you are going to have to play the prelude for me." I was horrified and began crying and pleading with her, "Mommy, I don't want to!" She was calm but resolute: "Kimberly, you *will* be on that piano bench and you *will* play the prelude." She also let me know that if I failed to do so, there would be serious consequences.

I made my way to the church, and seeing a full house that Sunday, timidly walked down the side aisle in an attempt to attract as little attention as possible. I was trembling with fear and embarrassment. My mind was racing with thoughts like, *what are all these people going to think when I start playing? I'm just a little kid! But I'm going to get a spanking if I don't do it!* It was quite the predicament for a little girl of my age and immaturity. I slid quietly onto the bench and began to play. Some of my anxiety eased when the music started flowing, and I gained a little courage when the ceiling didn't cave and the people didn't laugh. I even inserted a run here and there in the middle of a song, although I distinctly remember pushing the soft pedal each time I attempted it, just in case I missed a note or two. I also remember glancing furtively at the crowd to see if they had noticed the run I'd attempted.

That same year, dad came to me and asked if I wanted to go on a choir tour? He had put together a church choir which had gained some notoriety in our community, and had decided to take them on a music tour out west. He described the places we would visit along the way - Illinois, Missouri, Kansas, and then South Dakota. I had no idea where these places were, but it sure sounded like an exciting adventure. He told me that I would be playing the offertory each night, and I agreed to go mostly because the prospect of a road trip on a big bus sounded like so much fun. Perhaps God was preparing me early on for what He knew my life would be later.

That was also the year we lost our church organist. Mom, who played piano, moved to the organ and put me on the piano. Again, I was eight. I grew so much from this experience, but lacked confidence playing in certain keys. Mom explained to me that any time a song was written in D (two sharps), we would automatically transpose it to Db (five flats). I hated the key of Db, and remember asking our song leader one Sunday, "Bro. Voyles, *please* don't pick any songs written in five flats." Well, sure enough, he picked one in D (two sharps), which I knew I had to transpose to the *dreaded* key. I looked across the church at mom with panic on my face, but she resolutely stared me down and mouthed the words, "*Play it!*" I played it.

I played for congregational singing at my first camp meeting when I was eight years old as well. Dad was the evangelist, and our family was responsible for the special music. I'm not sure why mom put me on the piano, but perhaps she was simply busy with my younger siblings. Before service one evening, the song leader approached me and whispered kindly, "Kimberly, you're doing a great job! Just slow it down a little!"

It was somewhere around that same time when on a Sunday morning the choir stood to sing. Mom, the accompanist, had slipped out of the service to tend to one of my siblings. I was sitting on the front seat. I still remember the feeling of dread that washed over me as the choir director looked around trying to find his accompanist, and I heard someone whisper, "Kimberly can play this song!" Now, I knew in my heart that I could indeed play the song, but I was so shy that when dad looked at me with raised eyebrows, as if to say, "Kimberly, will you play?" I shook my head *vehemently*. Rather than embarrass me by pressing the issue, he let it go.

I remember feeling so worried that I would be in trouble for refusing to play, and that afternoon dad called me to his chair in the living room where he sat relaxing. He pulled me up onto his lap and spoke kindly and quietly, "Kimberly, you didn't want to play this morning, did you?" I shook my head, feeling nervous about my perceived disobedience. "Kimberly, God has given you a gift," he continued. There was no condemnation in his voice. "When you are given an opportunity, you should always play for Jesus." That was it! Nothing more was said. I was so relieved, and his tone and gentleness made me want to do just that. Play for Jesus.

One of the questions I'm most often asked is, "Where did you receive your musical training?" I have a slogan for it: On-the-Job Training, or more simply, OJT! No, my parents weren't remiss in seeking training for me. They hired piano teachers for several of us children, but I never excelled in lessons and frustrated my teachers to no end. I would watch and listen carefully as my teacher played the piece through, and then play it back while looking at her for approval. I can still hear her voice scolding, "Kimberly don't look at me, look at the notes! Thoroughly exasperated, she finally told my mother *not* to bring me back. She went on to say, "I have no idea what to do with this child."

The cessation of my formal music lessons only deepened my obsession with the piano. My mind was constantly fixated on chord structures and the melodies I could create using them. I remember riding down the road in the car and needing an outlet to express the sounds I was hearing in my head. In the absence of an actual keyboard, I simply created one using...*my teeth*! My two front upper incisors became, the left, B-flat, the wide space between, B-natural, and the right front tooth was C, and so on it went. I had a complete scale, and would play entire songs by tapping my teeth together. I heard every note and chord, and arranged many tunes this way. I know it sounds weird—it was weird—but such was my love of the piano.

I nearly failed my music theory class in the eighth grade because I had neither interest nor aptitude in learning the notes on the staff. My parents didn't stress out about this. We were a large ministry family, and my parents were engaged every day in caring for us, their congregation, and other ministries they were involved in. I was loved and nurtured as one of many. My parents included all of their children, and integrated us into everything they did. I am eternally grateful for the opportunities they provided for my siblings and me to hone our skills in practical and real-life situations.

It wasn't until I moved into my teenage years that I realized the importance of music theory. I was often invited to play for weddings, graduations, and other formal occasions, and when rehearsing for such events, I distinctly remember feeling *clueless* when the other trained musicians glibly called out names and types of chords. I'd scramble and figure out what they were talking about, but it *was* intimidating. I began checking out theory books from our local library and applying what I was playing on the keys to the theory behind it all. After marrying Phil, and having to accompany a church choir he directed, I learned to sight read. I took a few lessons, diligently applied myself, and today I can read music. I am a big supporter of education, and encourage young musicians to pursue learning the mechanics of music—even when their natural ear makes it difficult. I think this is important.

Throughout my life, I have been put in places where I have played piano in prestigious settings and in front of highly educated musicians. There have been times I have asked myself, *why did I not pursue a Bachelor's Degree in piano performance, a Master's Degree, even a Doctorate?* I grappled with this regret as a young woman, but today, I'm neither ashamed nor intimidated by this reality. God has helped me to see and accept that this was not *my* path. In His wisdom, *He's chosen* not to provide me these opportunities, and *I've chosen* not to question Him. And while I work hard to steward the gift God has entrusted to me, learn all I can, and push myself musically every single day, my greatest desire is that God receives all the glory.

In addition to pastoring, my father was a sought-after evangelist. Our family often traveled with him and provided special music. When I was ten, dad put together a trio made up of my older brother Jimmy and my two older sisters, Sandy and Vicky. I was the accompanist.

We were quite the group. There isn't a mild personality in our family! Dad was the boss. He picked our songs, arranged them, and oversaw each practice. My brother Jimmy was the comedian in the group, Sandy was the spiritual leader and the one who reminded Jimmy often that he needed to be serious about ministry. Vicky was most serious, and wanted to make sure we not only had our parts right, but that Jimmy didn't goof off too much and mess us up. I was the little kid on the piano just doing what I was told! The "Keaton Trio," as we were named, made an album when I was eleven and sold quite a few of those projects while traveling with our parents. On this album was my first ever recorded piano solo, "Down from His Glory."

Once, dad sent us alone for a weekend of singing in Georgia. *What was he thinking!?* This was a first—a *very memorable* first. Jimmy was sixteen and a new driver. We were living in Alabama at the time, and it was a long trip for three teenagers and a ten-year old. As we rolled down the highway in the 15-passenger van, I sat in the back and listened to the conversations taking place between my older siblings. I remember feeling quite concerned as Jimmy told Sandy he didn't feel like he was in a good place spiritually and that he wasn't prepared for ministry that weekend. *What!?* I remember Sandy rebuking him, and admonishing him: "*You need to pray, Jimmy!*" Our dad always impressed upon us children the importance of our service to God; that we should *never* take it for granted, but should *always* be prayerful and in a right relationship with the Lord. We siblings talked about this recently and had a good laugh about our immaturity, but even back then, we felt the weight and responsibility of ministry. Today, I could not be more thankful for this training.

That particular weekend was especially funny because the pastor asked Jimmy upon our arrival, "Jimmy, do you preach?" Jimmy had never preached a sermon in his life, but being the happy-go-lucky guy that he is, assured the pastor that he could indeed! Sandy panicked, while Jimmy scribbled some notes onto a piece of paper and delivered his first sermon, such as it was! Some years later, God did call Jimmy to preach, and he is a wonderful preacher/pastor today, pastoring in Hanover, PA.

Throughout my growing up years, I was very self-conscious about my piano playing, shrinking back from being the center of attention. I have vivid memories of a camp president coming to our cabin door and talking to dad. "I will pay Kimberly five dollars to play a piano solo for the evening service," he declared. These events always made me cringe and want to disappear. I loved playing the piano—more than anything in the world—but I was just a little girl, shy, and a bit of an introvert. While this personality sometimes collided with the expectations of others, my parents were my safe place, never making a big deal out of me or my piano playing. They *encouraged* me to *use* the gift I had for the Lord, but were careful not to exploit my gift for the sake of pleasing people. I knew they understood me and would always have my back. And, because they never made me feel bad about my reluctance to be up front, I overcame much of my backwardness as I moved into my teenage years.

When I was twelve, we moved to Westfield, Indiana, where my dad became the president of a Bible college and K-12 academy. This would not only be where I would complete middle school and high school, but where I would gain much more invaluable ministry experience as well.

Soon after we arrived on campus, I was called upon to accompany various vocal groups, the first being a college quartet. Throughout the school year, we traveled to represent the school, raise funds, and recruit students. My brother Jimmy sang lead, so traveling with four guys wasn't too uncomfortable for me. The music director for the college, and his wife, were accomplished and musically trained, and all of the music the guys were to sing was carefully chosen, written arrangements. The only problem was that I couldn't read the notes, and Mr. Overdorf wasn't sure how to teach me these arrangements, until one day I suggested, "Mr. Overdorf, why don't you play the song; I will listen and memorize it." He looked at me dubiously but agreed to try this approach. He would play the piece and then listen as I played it back from memory. When he stopped me to point out any discrepancy, I would make a mental notation, and move on. It worked beautifully. Looking back, I realize God was allowing me to form a mental discipline of memorization. I am often asked why or how I don't use written music, and I credit much of my ability to play from memory to those days of packing dozens of musical arrangements into my mind and performing them over and over again.

I won't forget the day Mr. Overdorf asked me, "Kim, do you have perfect pitch?" "What is that?" I replied. I had honestly never heard the term. He asked me to walk to the other end of the room and to turn my back to the piano. He then started playing notes and asking me to name them. I thought it was strange but quickly called out each one. I truly didn't understand his excitement upon discovering that he thought I did indeed have "perfect pitch". He told everyone he encountered about it, and it was embarrassing to me.

To this day, I'm not sure I understand exactly what perfect pitch means. I've known of people who could name each note after someone had pressed both hands and part of their arms down on the keys. If *that* is perfect pitch, I *certainly* do not have it! I do *not* enjoy pulling a note out of thin air to begin an a capella piece. I can do it, and occasionally have to, but I can be slightly off, especially if it's raining. I'm not sure why that is so. When it comes to the piano, however, I can walk into church on Sunday morning and know instantly what key the prelude is being played in, and can easily differentiate notes and keys that are being played.

My teenage years were full of adventure, for sure. I criss-crossed the country each summer visiting churches and youth camps with the quartet. We sang most weekends during the school year as well. These were good days, and I loved the music part of traveling, especially playing the piano. But I was often overwhelmed by loneliness and deep longings for home. I ached to be surrounded by the happy chaos of our large family, to sleep in my own cozy bed, to eat mom's delicious food at our large family table, or perhaps just to relax with a good book in the atmosphere of...home. The constant pressure and awkwardness I experienced when meeting new people and staying in the homes of strangers only added to my homesickness.

In those days, we would arrive at a church or campground, set up our sound system, perform our music, and then be assigned to a family for the night. As a thirteen and fourteen year-old girl, I would often look around and evaluate the different families present and secretly say to myself, *I wonder who I will be staying with tonight?* After having observed the various families in the church, I would think to myself, *that family looks nice, and they have little kids; I hope I get to stay with them.* Because I was the only girl in the group, I'd most often stay in a different place from the guys. There were really good situations, and some... not so good!

I recall, for instance, being placed in the home of an elderly hand-icapped lady. After enjoying a late night snack she had prepared for me, she directed me *outside*, and around the side of the house, where I climbed an outdoor staircase to an apartment above. I was absolutely *terrified*! After quickly changing into my pajamas, I climbed into bed and pulled the blankets up around me. It was then that I noticed the closet door slightly ajar, and in the shadowy darkness I was *sure* I saw a small casket in there!! I laid there *trembling* with fear until I finally drifted into an uneasy sleep. I never mustered up enough courage to check out the contents of that closet, though I'm quite sure it was no casket I saw, just creepy images formed by a young girl's fears!

Because I was sort of an "old soul" at twelve and thirteen, I was often treated like an adult in social situations. I dreaded being in someone's home after a service and being asked to play piano for the whole family. I don't fault anyone for this, because I know people just assumed I was confident and self-assured. I always did as I was asked, but deep down I longed to just sit in the room and blend in. Though my readers may find this hard to believe, I am by nature an introvert. As a young girl, I was content to sit on that piano bench, accompany the quartet, and be quiet. I would almost rather have *died* than opened my mouth to sing or speak. Sometimes, the oldest member and leader of our group would try to pressure me to give a testimony. This would completely stress me out, and I only remember cooperating one time. He wasn't too happy with me, but I was stubborn.

And there were a few occasions during my years of traveling as a teenager when I had had enough! The summer I was fourteen was especially hard; so hard that I believe I cried every single day. We were singing in Santoy, Ohio, and staying together in a two-story house, with my room just below the room where the quartet was staying. Hearing me crying through the floor one night, my brother Jimmy came down, sat quietly with me, and for once didn't have a funny comment or wisecrack to share. He sat there miserably, and finally stated, "This is ridiculous,

I'm calling dad tomorrow." I didn't argue. I was desperate for my family and the familiarity of home.

The very next morning, Jimmy pulled our travel van into an old gas station, called dad from the payphone, and handed me the receiver. I could barely get any words out through my tears. Hearing dad's voice was overwhelming. I just wanted to go home. Dad felt horrible. "Kimberly," He said, "I don't know who will play the piano for this group, but I assure you that I'm coming to get you and bring you home." To this day, one of the most beautiful sights I've ever seen was my dad pulling onto that campground, two days later, in his burgundy Oldsmobile 98. He brought a replacement for me, and she and I went to the camp tabernacle where I handed her a handwritten list of the repertoire and the appropriate keys for each song. I gave her a thirty-minute crash course on how each song was arranged, and then climbed into that beautiful car with my daddy and never gave that quartet another thought. I was going home!

During my last two years of high school, I traveled with a different quartet. These guys included my brother Jeff, Dan Coy, Mark Dubbeld (Mark Dubbeld Family) and sometimes Ray Cragun (The Craguns), who sang bass but didn't always travel. While the first quartet had been a group of college guys, this group was made up of high school students— very talented high school students. I shared many adventures with this group of guys as well. They were great, fun-loving, and took our ministry seriously—most of the time.

We typically traveled with a public relations employee from the school, and we traveled extensively during the summer and school year. In addition to scholarships for tuition, we were paid $10 a week during the summer, and $5 per service during the school year. I still have my pocket calendars from these years. It's astounding how busy we were, but those days taught me a lot about organization, time management, and financial stewardship.

I will never forget one night in Albuquerque, New Mexico with this high school group. Ray, our bass singer, wasn't with us, so it was just the three guys and me. We sang in a church on a Native American reservation. Afterwards, the pastor showed us to our rooms, and I was horrified when he took us to a large abandoned dormitory. It was dirty and full of old furniture and junk, but they had cleared out one room on the main floor and put a bed in it for me. On the second floor were two adjoining rooms which they had cleared for the guys. One had two beds in it and the other a couch. These were the kind of accommodations that nightmares are made of, and the ones I dreaded!

I prepared myself for bed, and had just started to drift off to sleep, when someone began banging on my window. I was frozen with fear. I couldn't move. I hoped and prayed that the guys were playing a trick on me, but the banging didn't stop. I listened intently to see if I could hear Mark's high-pitched, distinctive laugh, which would have been a dead giveaway. I heard nothing but the persistent *bang, bang, bang* on my window! Sheer terror propelled me out of that bed and to the door, where I crouched low to avoid being seen through the windows, and scuttled as quickly and carefully as I could through the large main floor room, which was a minefield of old beds, dressers, mattresses, and who knows what else... to the stairwell on the other side. I tore up those stairs and rapped loudly on the guy's bedroom door. I think I scared them half to death. They were not dressed, and came out with their bedsheets draped around them. And in this state of array, they, with a show of bravado, put me in the middle of them, (although I'm quite sure they were as frightened as I), and we all traipsed back downstairs to investigate. Our midnight visitor had fled, and we found no one. Of course, nothing could have compelled me to go back to my own sleeping quarters, so I spent the night in the adjoining room next to the guys. I slept on the couch, and my brother Jeff slept on the floor beside me. If my parents had only known! Thank God for my guardian angel and three teenage quartet boys.

From the vantage point of time, I reflect and am so grateful for these years and experiences. I realize that the events I have described in these pages were most unconventional; some might even say irresponsible. I would say that...it was a different time, a different day, a different culture in which we lived. And while I wouldn't have allowed my teenagers to travel in the same manner I did, I thank God that my parents' mindset during those days allowed *them* to allow *me* to do what I did. God used every one of those experiences to prepare me for my life's calling—one of sharing the Gospel through music around the country and throughout the world.

There are some specific things for which I am profoundly grateful:

I'm grateful that I gained a keen mindset for ministry. I learned that it's not just about the *music*. It's about the *message*! I was blessed. The guys I traveled with were wholesome, Christian young men. The Bible College we represented had a culture of living a life of prayerful carefulness before the Lord. We knew we needed God's help and anointing. I learned early on that seeking God does bring His help and blessing. I am forever impacted by the wonderful presence of the Holy Spirit that we witnessed during many of those services I described. God would come in direct answer to our prayers. He anointed the music, but more importantly, He anointed the *message* we delivered *through* that music. Today, I am so aware of the fact that without God's presence, the CFAM might as well sell the bus and stay home. I never, *never* want to do ministry without the help of the Holy Spirit.

I'm grateful that I learned practical wisdom about ministry. It sounds crazy to me now, but I remember crafting the schedule of our songs for upcoming services. I developed a sense of what worked and what didn't. I was observant, and picked this up from my dad. He had a gift for knowing what was appropriate musically in different settings. When I got it wrong, he would compliment my music, and then give gentle advice for the next time. I can remember approaching the leader of our group and making suggestions about how we might change the order of our program to make things flow better or build in a more effective way. I wonder how he felt about a young teenage girl giving him advice. Maybe he will read this account and let me know.

Today, this lesson is invaluable to our ministry. We pray about each concert; we walk onto the stage each night with a plan, but we've learned to stay tuned to the Holy Spirit to discern when the program needs to move in a different direction. Every audience is unique, every person loved by God, and we desire more than *anything* to be a channel through which his grace can flow.

I'm grateful that I gained a wealth of experience and developed musically. My travels as a young girl put me in countless churches and ministry settings that became the training ground I needed to prepare me for life. I had no way of knowing when I recorded an album at the age of thirteen that it would be the first of many. On three different occasions during my teenage years, I agreed to put on formal concerts, twice to raise funds for our school alumni association, and once for our senior class. It makes me smile remembering that I played for two hours and never spoke a word. Rob Hartman, the Vice President of the college, narrated between songs. He and I worked together for hours to blend his speaking with the music. I was a novice for sure, but we sold lots of tickets, and I think people enjoyed the evening.

I could not have foreseen that God would someday allow me to do full time concert ministry with my family. He is so good.

I'm grateful that I learned to depend upon God. I'm not trying to over spiritualize here, but traveling so much without my parents was tough. As I said before, I'm thankful for the opportunities I was given. On countless occasions, when lonely, afraid, or just tired of having to act like a grown up, I would talk to God. I didn't have a cell phone to FaceTime mom and dad before bed. How wonderful that would have been! When I was afraid, I prayed. When homesick, I prayed. When feeling insecure or uncertain, I prayed. And God heard those prayers.

Being a mother has caused me to look back and cringe on what could have happened to me in some of those places. I see so clearly that God's hand of protection never wavered for a moment. I have no horror stories to share. In all of those years of travel, not one nefarious deed was done to me.

Many years ago, Phil and I were ministering in a church where my dad was speaking for a series of services. We had provided some of the music for the weekend. One evening Dad said something in his introductory remarks that puzzled me. He said, "For many years I was known as Rev. Keaton, the evangelist, but today I am often referred to as the father of Kim Collingsworth." He looked down at me where I sat and said, "I have apologized to her for this." I sat there and thought to myself, *apologize?* I knew Dad was referring to my childhood. But I understood in that moment there was no need for apologies. My childhood had proved to be a blessing, though sometimes in disguise.

Recently, while talking over some of these details with my parents, my mom expressed aloud, (as she often does these days), "What were we *thinking!?*" It is true that from the viewpoint of today, we all see the uniqueness of my growing up years. Dad spoke up and said, "Sometimes when God calls someone to an uncommon life, he prepares them in uncommon ways." It was profound.

My parents are giants in my eyes. They demonstrated a simple faith and trust in God, and poured their lives into sharing the Gospel with the world around them. They taught each of my siblings and me to do the same. They showed us by example how to live out the Great Commission using the gifts God had given us.

While I rarely think about it, I guess it is true that many women aren't married to the kind of man who always has another seemingly impossible plan; most don't sleep on a bus 150 nights a year, eat dinner at midnight (sometimes) or not at all, stay up until 2:00 a.m. and sleep late. God knew just the kind of prepping I would need to live such a life, and He lovingly put me into the family I would need and gave me parents who would cooperate with His plan for me. I have been greatly blessed!

3

IT'S A CALLING, NOT A CAREER

It is the will of God that we are used in a ministry that is beyond us.
God calls us into a task that is way beyond our talent,
and that's when the Spirit comes in.
—Bishop Norman Wagner

Phil was born on May 3,1964, the youngest of three children and the only son. Unlike me, he was not born into a ministry family, but grew up on a quiet street in Dayton, Ohio. His family lived in a 1,075 sq. ft. frame home which his parents bought brand new shortly after they were married, and his father had returned from the Korean War. The neighborhood was humble, but respectable, and all the homes were pretty much identically the same. Many were purchased with provisions granted to war veterans upon their return home.

In this chapter, I've asked Phil to share his story in his own words.

I (Phil) have happy memories of long days spent playing with my friends in the neighborhood. Allen, David, Harold—the Brown boys across the street—and I had so much fun racing our bikes down the middle of the road in front of our houses. My huge collection of Matchbox cars was a neighborhood attraction, and my friends and I created elaborate towns cut out of felt (provided by my mom). We would play for hours out in the driveway. I have been told by my mom and sisters that

I was very *bossy*, and usually told everyone *what* we would play and *how* the games would go. Perhaps I was just trying to bolster my ego in a world of mothering sisters and mom!

I sometimes fought back as the "baby brother," and looked for ways to torment my sisters. I'm sure my older sister Rena still recalls the day I swiped her brand new "Chrissy" doll that she had just received as a treasured Christmas gift. Chrissy had hair almost the length of her body, and was unique because you could adjust the length of her hair by turning a knob on her back. I remember well, sneaking behind the couch with that doll and a pair of scissors. I turned the knob until the hair was as long as possible and then whacked it off! Facing the wrath of my sister was a fearsome thing when she returned from school, and I'm pretty sure I got a good spanking from mom too!

My mom was a godly, guiding force in my life for good. She grew up around the Christian Baptist denomination in southern Ohio, with a Christian mother, and had been saved as a young teenager.

Mom had many Christian influences in her life, including an uncle, the Rev. Sammy Sparks, who was a well-known evangelist in The Church of the Nazarene denomination. Mom loved to sing and had a nice voice. She sang in various mixed and ladies' trios as a teenager, and even traveled a bit singing for special services and camp meetings. For as long as I can remember, mom was the Sunday School song leader at our church. She took this job seriously and prayed earnestly about which song she should choose. In my mind's eye, I can still see the list of songs lying around the house throughout the week—a list she started on Monday morning as she wrote out possible selections for the following Sunday. She would pray about this throughout the week and systematically cross songs off the list until she had narrowed it down to the one she felt God wanted her to lead.

My dad was not a believer, and I only recall him going to church with us twice—once for an Easter service and once for a Christmas program. To be honest, this caused tension in our home and between my parents.

Mom was vigilant in her oversight of my sisters and me, and though she wouldn't have articulated it as such, she was diligent about crafting our worldview—a sound Biblical one. Dad had what we called the "TV room," where he spent hours in the evening and on weekends smoking his Camel cigarettes with no filters, and watching his favorite programs; this room we were *forbidden* to enter. He and mom must have had an understanding about this, as he went along with her on this rule. There were times when mom was gone that I'd stand up against the wall outside the "TV room" and watch an entire episode of *Adam 12*, my favorite popular police show at the time. Dad would call out, "*Phillip*, you *know* you're not supposed to be watching this."

Lest you think my mom was one who walked around with a "no" face, I believe she truly wanted what was best for us. She didn't feel television was a positive influence in our lives, but was very proactive, as well, about replacing it with wholesome and fun experiences all through my growing up years.

I thought my mom was great because she took us children *everywhere* she believed we would encounter positive spiritual influences. In the summertime we traveled to multiple church camps, arriving early for workdays, and staying late to assist with camp clean up. She took us to special services held at other churches, to revivals where anointed preachers would share God's Word, and to Gospel concerts where we would be exposed to great music.

She took me once to hear the great Duncan Campbell—the leader of the Great Hebrides Revival—and mom was so impacted by this man that shortly afterward, she and a few of her friends started regular cottage prayer meetings. I attended these with her as well. As a very young boy, I remember these ladies on their knees crying out to God for revival and for the salvation of their unsaved friends and family members. We children sometimes played *outside* during the meetings, but were aware of the importance of what was taking place *inside*. My mom was indeed a woman of prayer, and she believed in it's mighty influence. Even as a very young pre-schooler, I recall her established morning prayer routine once my sisters would leave for school. Not knowing what to do but wanting to be near my mom, I'd climb up on her back and fall asleep there, while she knelt and prayed. What precious memories!

Mom was also a generous supporter and proponent of Christian radio, and my sisters and I looked forward to listening to *Fables of Faith, Ranger Bill, Sailor Sam, Children's Bible Hour* and many other kid's programs after returning home from school and on Saturdays.

There were, of course, the regular three services a week at our own church, which we were faithful to attend. Our church was lively, and the music was quite loud and a bit fast. Our song leader, Jerry Hayden, played the trumpet while he led the singing. I loved that and determined, even as a 5-year-old, that I, too, would play the trumpet someday! When I began lessons in the fifth grade, I wasn't so excited to play in the band at school, but couldn't wait to play in the small church orchestra. After a semester of lessons, I was approved for both the band *and* the orchestra.

I loved unusual music as a small child. A traveling missionary came through who played the organ pedals, trumpet, and accordion all at the same time. I would sit on the edge of my seat in amazement, watching and listening to Leroy Adams. I witnessed many camp meeting services where God's presence would permeate the atmosphere during the special music. On one such occasion I was very young but I can still see Troy Cooke, a man crippled from polio, standing on the platform supported by arm braces, and singing *with passion* the words to a song penned by Mary J. Cartwright in 1889:

> I was drifting away on life's pitiless sea,
> And the angry waves threatened my ruin to be,
> When away at my side, there I dimly descried,
> A stately old vessel, and loudly I cried:
>
> "Ship ahoy! Ship ahoy!"
> And loudly I cried: "Ship ahoy!"

'Twas the "old ship of Zion," thus sailing along,
All aboard her seemed joyous, I heard their sweet song;
And the Captain's kind ear, ever ready to hear,
Caught my wail of distress, as I cried out in fear:

"Ship ahoy! Ship ahoy!"
As I cried out in fear: "Ship ahoy!"

The good Captain commanded a boat to be low'red,
And with tender compassion He took me on board;
And I'm happy today, all my sins washed away
In the blood of my Savior, and now I can say:

"Bless the Lord! Bless the Lord!"
From my soul I can say: "Bless the Lord!"

O soul, sinking down 'neath sin's merciless wave,
The strong arm of our Captain is mighty to save;
Then trust Him today, no longer delay,
Board the old ship of Zion, and shout on your way:

"Jesus saves! Jesus saves!"
Shout and sing on your way: "Jesus saves!"

As the believers in the room worshipped, identifying with the allegory of lost sinners being rescued from destruction by Jesus and the power of the Gospel, something rose up within my heart. The blending of poetic metaphor with a beautiful melody and a poignant message moved me powerfully in a way I didn't even fully understand as a child.

I gave my heart to Jesus on a Wednesday evening in 1970. Our pastor, Rev. Walter Hobbs, preached a sermon on the Second Coming of Christ. Though I was a mere six years of age, the Holy Spirit spoke to my young heart, and for the first time I became aware of my need for salvation. I knew in my heart I wasn't ready should Christ return that night, and when the invitation was given, I went forward, knelt at the altar, and asked Jesus to save me. I knew He did, and that's where my relationship with Christ began.

I sang my first solo in church when I was about five years old. Mom put me up on a Sunday evening, and I sang in a high and strong chest voice, "The Darker the Night, the Brighter the Light Shines." I sang this with my sisters at our church camp meeting that summer as well, and took the tenor part. Mom was approached by a man, Rev. Bill Fannin, who had a program on a radio station in Springfield, Ohio, and we ended up traveling there to sing on the radio. It was exciting—my first over-the-road singing engagement and, perhaps, an early indication of things to come!

Mom also bought a Baldwin piano and was determined that my sisters and I would all learn to play. My sister Connie became accomplished, and is a church pianist and music teacher today. My sister Rena took to it naturally and accompanied a quartet in college. I hated every minute of these lessons, but they did force me to learn to read music and play a little. My motivation to learn in spite of my dislike for piano was partly due to a chewing out I received when I was merely five years of age. My sweet teacher, JoAnn Hobbs, *really* let me have it one week when it became obvious that I hadn't spent a moment practicing. I had never seen this side of her, and it made me cry. I sat there with tears rolling down my cheeks as she calmly handed me a Kleenex and continued her lecture! I was devastated that I had let her down and never, ever came unprepared to a lesson again.

Mom was an avid vinyl records collector. We owned every album The Speer Family, The Rambos, Henry and Hazel Slaughter, The Bill Gaither Trio, The Lanny Wolfe Trio, and many others produced. She was a member of the Berean Club, and would go to their monthly meetings and bring home the latest Gospel music album on the market. I can still remember excitedly slitting open the end of a new album, tearing off the cellophane wrapper, and sitting in the living room soaking up the harmony. Mom was partial to mixed groups, so I don't recall us ever owning a quartet album.

I was thrilled when, on my fourteenth birthday, my parents bought me a nice stereo for my room, along with a great pair of headphones. I had never owned anything like this before and spent hours in my room listening to the best and latest Gospel music available.

One evening, during my freshman year of high school, I lay on my bed gazing at the ceiling while listening to a brand-new live album entitled, *Henry and Hazel, Just the Way We Are*. On this particular record, their daughter and two sons joined them with both vocals and instruments. The sweet family harmony was not lost on me, and something... something divine and life-changing happened in my spirit as I listened. I found myself so profoundly moved by the music that I began to weep. And then I felt confused and overcome by the emotions I was experiencing. I got down beside my bed, buried my head in my hands, and began to pray. "God, what is happening?" I asked. "Why am I crying?" As I knelt there, God spoke to me, not in an audible voice, but in my spirit. I felt...heard him say, "Phil, *this* is what I want you to do. You're going to sing with your family."

That was an amazing, defining moment in my life and set the compass for every step I would take going forward. I was focused and knew from that moment what I was going to do with my life. I had been called and chosen by God to sing, *with a family!*, and I couldn't *wait* to fulfill that calling.

It was around this time that I decided I wanted to go away to a Christian boarding school in Cincinnati. My sisters had left home already and attended God's Bible School and College, located in the Queen City. Life had gotten tough for me at home, and I wanted to get away. There were a few obstacles preventing me from going, the first and most daunting being my father. Allow me to give a little background.

Dad was from Wheelersburg, Ohio, and did not have a Christian upbringing, nor had he been exposed to many Christian influences. He altered the truth a bit on his age, and joined the army at seventeen. He was almost immediately shipped off to fight in Korea with the 24th Infantry Division of the 52nd Field Artillery Battalion.

When dad was nineteen, his division was near the Kum River in Korea, when the 19th Regimental Combat Team, to which his Division was attached, was overrun by overwhelmingly large enemy forces. According to official records,

> Private Collingsworth approached the senior officer present and volunteered to undertake any duty assigned to him. In the face of withering enemy fire, he assisted in rallying drivers, in overturning wrecked vehicles blocking the road, and in moving unattended vehicles that were impeding progress. He volunteered to man a machine gun on one of the vehicles, and when the driver in front of him abandoned his quarter-ton-truck, Private Collingsworth cooly took over. Private Collingsworth drove skillfully and courageously, refusing to stop even when other vehicles did so. He drove through three islands of enemy resistance in his break for safety. By this daring coolness and gallantry, Private Collingsworth assisted materially in extricating a group of completely surrounded men from certain annihilation.

Dad was awarded the silver star by President Harry Truman for his "gallantry" and for "bringing such high credit to himself and to the military."

I can still recall lifting the lid of my mom's cedar chest which held all of his war memorabilia. As a child, I would carefully look through the items there—I was proud of my father, although he never shared any of his experiences with me. The scent of that cedar chest represented to me, my dad, the war hero.

I'm not sure why our relationship deteriorated as I moved into my teenage years. I have many happy memories with my dad as a small boy. Sometimes he'd take a day off work just to take me fishing. On one such fishing expedition to Eastwood Lake, I remember bringing home thirty-two crappies. Many times, on Saturday, dad would take me to Vandalia, Ohio to see my grandfather. Grandpa lived on a farm and had a beautiful, yellow Cub Cadet tractor that he'd let me drive through the green fields. I cherish the memory of my grandpa gently extracting my foot caught in the chicken wire as his chickens pecked my bare toes and I screamed in fear.

Dad always got paid by General Motors on Friday's, and when I was a young boy he'd stop and cash his check at Diamond Drugstore on his way home from work, and then pick a brand-new Matchbox car up for me. I had a few hundred of these beauties by the time I was ten years of age, making me the envy of my neighborhood friends.

I don't know exactly when it happened, or why, but Dad's attitude toward me began to change as I grew into a young man. Was it because my interest didn't meet his expectations? Did it have something to do with my Christian faith? I still do not understand it to this day, but as I began to grow into a young man, I became the object of dad's ridicule. It was unspeakably painful for me. I believe my dad loved me, but I didn't feel his love as a teenage boy.

When I was a freshman in high school and expressed a desire to attend God's Bible School the following year, Dad was furious. And his fury became an obstacle to the fulfillment of this desire. Finances became a huge problem, not because my parents couldn't afford it (dad had a great job at GM, and we lived comfortably), but because my dad declared he would "*never* pay a *dollar*" for me to go to that school!

My mom was aware of the toxic relationship between dad and me and believed the Christian environment of a Bible school would be good for me. Though she had never really worked outside our home, mom was determined to make my dream happen, so she got a paper route, delivering more than 300 papers a day to help pay my way.

Even with this job, however, I would still need to be approved for a work scholarship, but I learned that the school only awarded these scholarships to older students. The school also had a policy that they would only accept boarding students who were at least in their junior year of high school. I was a freshman, and the thought of waiting another year was dismal. I am so grateful for people God placed in my life to help get me to God's Bible School.

I was attending a private Christian school at the time, and one of my teachers, a single lady by the name of Ms. Elaine Nicholas, was instrumental during this crucial time in my life. I confided in her my desire to go away to school. She listened, was supportive of the idea, and when I asked if she thought it possible for me to complete two years of high school in one to expedite my going, she didn't even blink. She set about making a plan for me to do so. She mapped out my freshman year and the summer following. She tutored me for three hours a day in math and science, which included Physical Science and Trigonometry. God placed Ms. Nicholas in my life; she invested in me, and I am forever grateful!

There were several from our church who believed I was much too young to leave home, and told my mother so. But Ms. Nicholas supported my mom, and in her quiet way was adamant as she admonished me, "Phillip, go to God's Bible School. It will change your life!" She is retired now after spending most of her career teaching Greek to many young people training for the ministry. She never married or had children of her own, but there are many men and women sharing the Gospel around the world today because of her diligent and sacrificial service. A few years ago, she attended a Collingsworth Family concert. It made my night to see her there, and I had the opportunity to thank her again for giving a young man a helpful shove in the right direction.

My other reason for wanting to make sure I could go to GBS for my junior year was because I was determined to be valedictorian of my class, and knew I would need to have attended their high school for at least two years to be eligible.

I applied for the work scholarship, which would pay the remaining portion of my room and board, and was devastated when I was denied because of my age.

Shortly after being denied, the college choir from God's Bible School came to our church for a performance. I attended the concert and was so moved by the music that my desire to attend this school became even more overwhelming. The vice president of the school was there that night. He was new to the job, and I had never met or spoken with him before. I had no way of knowing *then* how our lives would intersect in the future. Something about his demeanor impressed me. He seemed kind and approachable, so I decided to write him a letter.

That very week, I sat at the table and wrote out a handwritten appeal to Vice President James Keaton. I expressed my desire to attend God's Bible School. I told him I had been turned down for the scholarship; a scholarship I desperately needed, not because my parents couldn't afford it, but because my father wasn't willing to pay. Two weeks later, I received a personal response from Rev. Keaton. He told me that while I was "technically not eligible for the scholarship," he was going to work it out and grant me one. His reason? "When I was a fourteen-year-old young man, someone made it possible for me to attend Bible school, and it changed my life." He wanted to do his part to pay it forward. I was ecstatic!

I had no way of knowing then that this man who helped change the entire trajectory of my life would someday become my father-in-law, though I wouldn't have the opportunity to meet him again for several more years. He only spent one year at God's Bible School, and when I arrived, their family had moved to a different state. It is astounding to me the ways in which God weaves people and events into the narrative of our lives to bring about his purposes.

Now, back to my father. He never understood my love and pursuit of music. He thought I was smart and wanted me to be an attorney. He couldn't comprehend the whole Bible school desire. "Music is stupid," and, "You will starve if you pursue this dream," he said. I know now that he just couldn't see with spiritual eyes. He didn't understand or appreciate the calling God had placed in my heart.

Truthfully, I am probably more like my dad than I know. The same drive and determination that prodded him to take charge on the battlefield as a nineteen-year-old, is probably what made me determined as a fifteen-year-old to escape the derision, and prove to him I would do something with my life—even if that something was completely different from what he wished for me. I *did* long for my dad's approval. Doesn't every young man? And, I see now that my resolve back then to be valedictorian (which I did achieve), was partly born out of the slightest glimmer of hope that dad would notice and be proud.

I moved to Cincinnati and into the men's dormitory in time to start my junior year in high school, made friends quickly, and stayed busy with schoolwork and my work scholarship responsibilities. I earned every bit of my room and board by cleaning the large college chapel auditorium. Sweeping and mopping the old wooden floors three times each week was a back breaking job, but I was grateful to be there. GBS was a busy place. I had wonderful teachers and enjoyed my classes. I did miss my mom—and her cooking—terribly. My weight dropped from 165lbs to 132lbs during that first year. At six feet one inch, I was a skinny kid!

I was glad when the manager of the campus bookstore requested me as her assistant the following year, and I found working in the bookstore to be a bit less physically strenuous than housekeeping. I helped to order new books and music, worked on shelf displays, and ran the cash register. It was while working there that I became aware of an album we often played in the bookstore. It was one called "The Keaton Trio." I knew these were the children of the same Rev. Keaton who had been responsible for my coming to God's Bible School. On this album, the youngest in the group, an eleven-year-old girl named Kimberly, played a piano solo. I remember thinking as I listened to her play, "Down from His Glory," *Wow, she plays really well for an eleven-year-old, but she sure plays fast!*

I spent seven wonderful years at God's Bible School and College, although I came close to changing my life's direction after high school.

Towards the end of my senior year in high school, I was given the opportunity to audition for a college male quartet which would be traveling throughout the summer, representing the school. I knew that I needed to be in this quartet as it came with a great scholarship. In my mind, I put out a fleece to the Lord. "God, if you really do want me to have a music career, I need to stay here, and I need that scholarship."

I auditioned before the music directors for just a few minutes before being excused. There were others who were called back to the audition room several times. I was not. I went to my room thinking I certainly would not be chosen for the group. I lay on my bed and thought about my alternate plan. I would return to Dayton, attend a local community college, and study finance. Perhaps I would choose a career in banking. Then my roommate came in a bit later and told me my name was on the quartet list. I had been chosen to sing; I was shocked. And, I was thrilled. This was just another way God redirected my mind to the call He had given me years before.

Criss-crossing the country, singing in hundreds of churches and Bible camps would be my life for the next five summers. This opportunity came with a great scholarship that took care of my college expenses. In addition to the quartet, I also toured each year with both the orchestra and college choir, and additionally was chosen to be the assistant choir director in my senior year. I discovered during college that I could play the organ better than I had played the piano. I was recruited, and played for chapel each week, as well as played duets with the choir pianist on all of our tours. When I received my diploma, I laid down my career as an organist, and though Kim has tried on occasion to get me to play, I'm content to leave the keys to her.

I am so grateful for the time I spent at God's Bible School and College. I completed my college years with a dual major in trumpet performance and music education. It was a time in my life that deepened my walk with the Lord. It was an extension of the Biblical foundation laid by my mother and church family back home. The required Bible courses gave me more love for God's Word. I also heard Biblically sound preaching from well-known visiting theologians, such as Dr. Dennis Kinlaw, Dr. Ross Lee, Dr. Wingrove Taylor, and many others.

My college years at GBS were not merely about obtaining a degree. All of my experiences combined have proved invaluable to my life. God knew when He spoke to my heart at the age of fourteen just what I needed to propel me on that path. I needed a God-focused environment, godly mentors, a strong work ethic, opportunities to hone my spiritual gifts and musical skills, and so much more.

Specifically, I learned the absolute necessity of building a network of friends, pastors, and ministry leaders as the infrastructure of an operational ministry.

I watched with fascination as Larry and Tricia Jewett (the college's Public Relations Director) used their many years of contacts in song evangelism and music ministry to secure venues and locations for our quartet to sing all over the US and Canada. I caught this almost unwittingly, as I couldn't have known what our ministry would look like today. Their advice and influence at this very critical time in my life can only be seen as monumental and timely.

The chair of our music department, Garen Wolf, wasn't a physically large man, but he was a *giant* in my life. He was passionate about everything he did. He was so loved by his choir and orchestra members, although he was rigid in his expectations of each of us. He emphasized, continually, the standard of excellence with which the musicians in the Old Testament tabernacle were measured—that they were paid, and that their positions were a vital part of worship. He hammered the truth to us that we would not be held to any lower standard of excellence. This impacted me, and I determined that I would be faithful to do my very best for God's glory.

In this environment, surrounded by people who valued music, I was able to truly embrace God's calling and prepare myself for music ministry. I'm indebted to those who stepped into my life, mentored me, believed in me, and prayed for me. People like Paul and Donna Peak, David and Martha Miller, Fred Wingham, Kenneth Stetler, Joe Brown, Delbert Walker, Archie Coons, Jewel Smith, Saralynne Clouse, Herman and Marilyn Noll, Archie Atwell, Marcia Davis, and a huge host of others whose influence I still refer back to, to this day.

Reflecting over my early life has been good for me. Pausing to think upon God's sovereignty so deliberately woven through every time and season is life giving—even though some of those seasons are still particularly painful for me to remember.

In November of 2005, after putting up a brave fight lasting six years, my mom succumbed to ovarian cancer. As I stood with my sisters at her graveside, I felt both sorrow and profound gratitude—gratitude that I was blessed with such a mom—one who introduced me to Jesus, and who took her responsibility as a godly mother seriously. I also thanked God that she lived to witness God's answer to her deepest prayer—the one for my dad's salvation.

It was about one year into her cancer journey that she was too ill to attend church on a Sunday morning. Dad got up, got dressed, and went to church without her. He had in recent months been softening toward God. He had attended occasionally with mom, but had made no profession of faith. Later that morning my mom received a phone call from one of her church friends, Ruth Ann—a lady mom had been praying with for years. She said excitedly into the phone, "Billie, Ray is at the altar praying to be saved!" It was a wonderful day! These faithful believers had been praying for my dad for decades. This friend of mom's couldn't even wait for church to be dismissed to share the news with her. The Word of God is true when it states, *"Surely the arm of the Lord is not too short to save, nor his ear too dull to hear" (Isaiah 59:1-2,NIV).* He had heard and had reached out His loving arm and answered our prayers. And my mom had a front row seat.

Dad's conversion did change him. I won't forget the day, when preparing to leave my parent's house after a visit, I began to lead our family in a parting prayer. Shortly into my prayer, dad's big voice cut in as he took over and began to pray for *us.* Kim says I went silent, and she peeked to see a stupendous look of incredulity on my face. I had never heard my dad pray *any* kind of prayer in 36 years of living. It was beautiful!

For the next five years, mom battled cancer, and dad's health declined as well. He suffered from COPD (an inflammatory lung condition) and emphysema, and required oxygen most of the time.

Shortly after mom's death, I went to visit him. He lived alone in a small apartment within an assisted living facility. I noted his condition was deteriorating rapidly. Seeing him old and frail and short of breath was particularly tough for me. I loved my dad, and though our relationship had been so difficult, it had been somewhat better in recent years.

I took with me that day a copy of our latest DVD titled, "Christmas in Kosovo." The previous year, The Collingsworth Family had been invited by the US government to visit Camp Bondsteel in Kosovo and sing for the troops on Christmas Eve and Christmas Day. This DVD documented that trip and the music we had shared. I'm not exactly sure why I brought the DVD with me, except that I knew an important part of my dad's identity had been wrapped up in his military service. And even though he had never understood my calling as anything other than a poor career choice, I wanted to share this with him.

I sat beside him and turned it on, and we watched it together. As the DVD played, dad sat with tears running down his face. When it was finished, he turned and looked at me and with a trembling voice said, "Son, I want you to know that I am proud of you; I'm proud of your family and what you are doing."

I was 41 years old. I had learned to embrace God as my father—especially in the absence of a close relationship with my earthly one. But even as I share this with the reader today, the emotion of that moment with my dad is overwhelming. I didn't expect to ever hear those words from him. They were a gift to me, and remain so to this day.

My dad died a month later, just over three months after the death of my mom.

I know I will see them both again!

When I look back over my life, with all its twists and turns, I stand amazed at God's ability to make music of one's life—of my life—however discordant things may have seemed at times. He is the Master Artist blending the bright and dark colors of our lives into a painting of his delight. And he is the Master Conductor who tunes the music of our lives into melodies that bring glory to His name. No matter how painful your story, He wants to make music of your life too! As our friends Bill and Gloria Gaither put it,

> Something beautiful, something good,
> All my confusion he understood;
> All I had to offer him was brokenness and strife,
> But he made something beautiful of my life.[1]

---

1 Bill and Gloria Gaither, *Something Beautiful*, Gaither Music, 1971

4

HOW WE MET

If music be the food of love, play on.
—Shakespeare

I met Phil on Friday evening, August 26, 1983. I was fourteen and going into the ninth grade. Phil was nineteen and beginning his sophomore year in college.

Our meeting was a providential encounter, and my life would never be the same.

I wasn't a typical fourteen-year-old when it came to boys. I had never had a serious boyfriend or even been more than mildly interested in the opposite sex. I was busy traveling, playing piano, and trying to keep up with my schoolwork, and guys just weren't very interesting to me. I was rather shy and somewhat introspective, and most of the time I didn't even notice if they were paying attention to me. When I did notice, I did everything in my power to avoid uncomfortable interactions.

Once when our family was providing the preaching and music for a church camp, a certain young man developed an interest in me. He was quite aggressive, and even asked if I would sit with him in church. I was horrified, embarrassed, and wanted nothing to do with him! So when he parked himself just outside our trailer one evening, waiting for me to exit, I was furious. I was only twelve or thirteen but exhibited my stubborn side by telling my family, "I will *not* be going to church *or* play-ing the piano until someone makes him disappear." My brothers teased me and mom felt sorry for him, telling me that, "It wouldn't hurt to sit with the poor guy." I was finally taken seriously, and one of my brothers got rid of him for me. I'm sure he was perfectly nice, but I wasn't ready for those kinds of relationships, however benign.

I had no way of knowing on that Friday evening in August of 1983 that I was to be the victim of a *massive* set-up. I had never heard of Phil Collingsworth—had never heard him sing, and although we had both been traveling in singing groups for two "sister" colleges, our paths had never crossed. I found out later that he had traveled primarily on the West Coast each summer, while I had been mostly covering the Midwest and Eastern part of the US.

That evening, a high school friend of mine and I were invited by our principal's wife on a shopping trip for an upcoming high school event. Hope Welbaum was not just the principal's wife, but a fun-loving lady whom we all liked. She and I had developed a friendship, so I went along to enjoy the evening. What I didn't know was that Hope was also a child-hood friend of Phil's, and that she and Phil's sister, Connie, were deter-mined that Phil and I would meet. She knew Phil had come to Westfield, Indiana, to visit his sister for the weekend before starting classes the fol-lowing Monday in Cincinnati. When she casually mentioned we were stopping by Connie's house, I thought nothing of it. I stayed in the car until Hope returned and insisted that I come inside and meet a friend of hers, Phil Collingsworth. My first response was "*No,*" but she persisted, and I reluctantly followed her inside.

That first meeting was a bit uncomfortable. Phil and I approached one another as Connie said, "Kim, meet *the* Phil Collingsworth!" We awkwardly said hello, and *more* awkwardly shook hands! Things kind of spiraled out of control when Connie and Hope both insisted we play a pi-ano/trumpet duet. I kept my composure and tried my best to politely de-cline, but Phil was up for it, and the merry *matchmakers* wouldn't relent.

Phil asked me what I wanted to play, and I mumbled, "I don't care, you choose." He suggested a Gaither classic, "Because He Lives," in the key of B-flat. As soon as my fingers touched the keys I was in my element, and the awkwardness dissipated. I played...and listened, appreciating his skill. I remember thinking this was kind of fun but when it was over, I was ready to *go*. We said goodbye, and my heart did a little flip when Phil winked at me after walking me to the door.

I must admit I was impressed. Phil was handsome, winsome, and he obviously loved music. He was on my mind for the rest of that evening, and I kept thinking, "*why did he wink at me? This guy has audacity!*" I never let on to my friends there was anything special about the meeting.

The very next day, Hope called again and wasn't quite as subtle as the day before. She had arranged for Phil and me to meet at a local church to "do music" together. She assured me Phil was a great organist, and that I would love hearing him play. I agreed to go. Phil and I spent the evening playing through the hymnbook, me on piano, and him on the organ. Once again, it was an enjoyable experience. He was a talented musician. When we said goodbye, he expressed regret that he would be unable to come and hear my quartet the following morning, as he would be attending another church in town with his sister.

He changed his mind!

The next day as I entered the church where we were to sing, much to my surprise I spotted Phil, impeccably dressed and standing in the foyer. He smiled at me and said, "Hi, Kimmy!" I bolted to the bathroom to compose myself and thought, *Kimmy? What in the world is happening? This guy is up to something!* We spoke briefly at the end of the service, and when he found that we were to be singing in Cincinnati that evening (150 miles away), he again expressed regret that he wouldn't be able to attend due to other obligations.

That evening, just before our service began, I glanced up and—you guessed it—Phil Collingsworth was standing in the foyer. I went into full-blown panic mode. *Okay, this guy is stalking me!* was my first thought. I surrounded myself with people after the service and made it impossible for Phil to approach me. I was young, nervous, and although very interested in him, I felt a bit of pressure. And I knew I would be teased mercilessly by the quartet guys. This, coupled with the foreign feelings swirling around in my heart, only accentuated my need for space.

I'm glad Phil wasn't easily deterred. I'll pause here and let you read his perspective on that most momentous weekend.

My (Phil) sisters were notorious for trying to help me along in the area of romance, and I was accustomed to their attempts to match me up.

I had dated a couple of girls in college but knew that neither was right for me. For some reason, I instinctively knew that in order to fulfill God's call on my life I *had* to marry a piano player. So each time Connie regaled me with the attributes of the latest female she had in mind for me, my first question was always, "Does she play the piano?" If the answer was "No," I wasn't interested. That may seem strange to some, but I believe it was God's way of putting Kim and me together.

On this particular weekend, Connie had three girls lined up for me to meet. Honestly, I wasn't looking forward to it at all and assumed they would all be "duds"! (My sister did *not* have a good track record in setting me up.) I asked the customary question about each girl's ability on the piano. Connie assured me they all played well but that one of them played "*extraordinarily* well." She failed to mention that *that* girl was only *fourteen years old!*

How well I remember meeting Kim. She was mature, somewhat shy, very pretty, with beautiful brown eyes and dark hair. She looked and acted older than her fourteen years (her age was a detail I wouldn't discover until later). And when she sat down to play—well...it was amazing. As soon as her fingers began to move across the keyboard, I knew instinctively that she was a natural musician—an artist—and I was instantly captivated by this girl. What a gift she had, and those other girls disappeared from my thoughts forever!

As Kim has written, I showed up everywhere she was for the rest of that notorious weekend. I was a little frustrated when I left the church on Sunday night. I knew she had avoided me, but honestly, I wasn't discouraged in the least. I had never felt such a strong attraction to a girl. And I knew there was an undeniable chemistry between us.

I traveled back to my dorm, sat at my desk, and wrote her a letter. I put Kim's name, but my sister's address on the envelope, as I didn't have Kim's address at the time. I didn't want to wait until the following day to post it, so I sneaked out of the dorm just before midnight and drove into downtown Cincinnati. I knew there were mailboxes that were emptied and processed every hour on the hour. As I recall, when I arrived there was a mail carrier emptying the box. I placed the letter in his bin and returned to my room feeling satisfied that I had done all I could do in one day. I closed my eyes and slept with visions of a sweet and most intriguing young lady filling my mind.

When I (Kim) walked into choir practice on Tuesday, Phil's sister began waving an envelope in my direction. "Look what I have!" she said with a laugh. I felt my face flush! I took the envelope she offered and shoved it into my pocket and out of sight without saying a word. I went to the piano bench, gained my composure, and tackled the songs we were practicing that day.

As soon as I left the choir room, I found a private place and opened the envelope addressed to "Kim Keaton." The following is Phil's very first letter to me, and the beginning of a friendship that would blossom into romance:

> Dear Kim,
>
> I imagine you're surprised to get a letter from me.
>
> How is school going for you? I hope that Mrs. Hilligoss is not being too hard on you all. I imagine she'll be a good teacher.
>
> I wanted to ask you Sunday if I could write to you but did not get the chance to. I asked _____ (a mutual friend) if she

thought that you would mind, she said that she wasn't sure but that I could try it so that's what I'm doing.

Maybe you're liking someone, I don't know, well anyway you can let me know. If you would rather I didn't write or if your parents don't allow it, just let me know. I'll try my best to be good. (ha)

I sure enjoyed my visit there over the weekend at the school. I was impressed with the student body, there is so much talent and potential there.

I think the Lord must have sent your dad there just at the right time. God's hand must surely be on the school. The quartets were really great, especially the piano player for the first quartet. I enjoyed it all. Keep tickling those ivories.

Oh, it was also fun to play the piano and organ together. It's not often I get to play with someone so accomplished.

I guess I should ask you if you'd rather be called "Kim", or "Kimberly"? I'm sure you probably don't want to be called Kimmy. I remember calling you that and then thinking that you probably wouldn't like that.

Better go for now. I think we are going to have a good school year. It's pretty crowded but we're making it.

I hope Connie gets this to you ok. I didn't know your address since you aren't living at the school anymore, so I just sent it to her house.

Bye, See ya! (Write me back)
Phil Collingsworth
1810 Young St.
Cincinnati Ohio

I wasted no time in returning his letter, and he received mine on Thursday of the same week:

Phil,

Hello! I received your letter this afternoon and to say the least, I was surprised. School is good so far. This is only my fourth day and so I'm in the process of getting adjusted again, especially since they just put this new system in.

I would be happy for you to write to me. Of course, there is no problem with my parents at all.

I'm really glad you enjoyed the quartets this weekend. I think the first quartet was a little nervous to sing in front of you. Really, I can see why.

Oh, thanks for the compliment about the piano playing also. I sure can't say that I am an accomplished pianist at all but with the Lord's help, I do try.

By the way, I think I would rather be called "Kim" than anything and for sure, not "Kimmy". Ha! I really wondered what you meant by calling me that Sunday.

Well, I guess I need to sign off and get busy on my homework. Thanks for writing,

Kim

Seven letters and two weeks later, Phil called and made an appointment with my father's secretary to speak with him by phone. He asked permission to visit and attend the upcoming school revival. He told dad about his interest in me. Dad agreed we could write letters and visit with one another in a group setting, and Phil was happy with that.

Phil drove from Cincinnati to attend the revival, and arrived just before the service. Dad greeted him and asked if he would be willing to sing a solo just before the message. Dad was very presumptuous and assured Phil that I would "be *glad*" to accompany him on the piano. We had only moments to discuss the song and key, and no time at all for rehearsal. The auditorium was packed that night, and the pressure was palpable for both of us. I played for worship, and a special for the offertory, and scarcely had time to think about our upcoming "debut." Dad introduced Phil, and we were on.

The song Phil chose that night was one he had sung many times. "He Will Not Fail Me Now," was written in 1926 by Bessie Hatcher. I knew it well. I had never heard Phil sing, but the way he sang with confidence in his signature rich baritone voice was moving and beautiful. I slipped in a half-step key change between the second and third verse, and it was as if we had always been making music together. The most memorable aspect of that evening, however, was the way God's presence settled down during the song. There were seekers at the altar, and a spirit of worship filled the room. As I played and Phil sang, I knew (as much as a fourteen-year-old girl can know) that this was "right." From where I sat on the piano bench, I had a perfect view of my dad's face. He knew it too.

As for Phil, he declares he had already decided to marry me!

That evening after the service, mom and dad took Phil and me out to Perkins. Mom was her sweet, unassuming self, and made Phil feel welcomed and right at home. Dad was kind and gracious, but he also had a way of keeping Phil just a bit off balance. I was awkward and just wanted the evening to be over. While my older sisters were comfortable around guys, and had had boyfriends to spare, this was way out of my comfort zone. There was something very special about Phil, however, and I wanted to continue our correspondence.

Right about now, I can imagine many of my readers have stopped breathing! You're probably wondering about a 14-year-old girl beginning a romance with a 19-year-old college student, and about the parents who would allow it. As I reflect on it from the vantage point of time, maturity, and cultural shifts, it almost takes my breath away too.

This *is* our story, however, and I'm not ashamed of it. My parents married very young, and in the time and culture in which we were raised this was not uncommon or frowned upon.

The weekend I just described was the beginning of a relationship that would span the next three years. I still have more than three hundred letters received from Phil during those years. We also talked on the phone each week, and Phil fed countless rolls of quarters into payphones from all over the US just so we could stay in touch. I can still hear his, "Hang on Kim, I'm running out of time," as the operator threatened to disconnect our calls.

Phil's first visit to our home had me feeling a little anxious, to say the least. There were still seven of us children living at home, and I wanted a perfect evening. My younger siblings, especially Julia and Brian, four and eight at the time, could be unpredictable, and I just *knew* they'd embarrass me in some way. Phil remembers being more than a little overwhelmed by the sheer volume of people and the multiple conversations happening all at once. He was accustomed to a quiet, orderly, and structured environment. Our home was loud, and Phil admits he wasn't prepared for the chaos!

Phil still jokes about the "Keaton family kitchen trash can." He had never known a home where the trash needed to be taken out so often, nor did he understand how so much could be stuffed into one can! He declares that my mom's welcoming personality and her intentional conversations with him saved the day.

On one of his first visits, Phil suggested we try singing together. Now, you must understand that sitting on the piano bench and accompanying others was as natural as breathing for me, but singing...? This was something foreign and a little intimidating. Other than singing with my entire family, I had rarely ever sung in public, and had certainly never sung a duet with anyone. I pushed down the rising apprehension and agreed to try. From the very beginning, Phil had the ability to draw me out in ways others had been unable to do. And I see now that Phil was just being Phil—brilliant at seeing potential, and always looking down the road envisioning what could be.

Once again we chose a Gaither classic, "This Could Be the Dawning of That Day." Phil took the lead, and I harmonized with him. Our voices blended, and some of my timidity began to evaporate as I, for the first time, "found" my singing voice. Several of my siblings drifted into the room to listen, and I think they were as shocked as I was to hear me singing.

It was one thing to sing together in the safety and comfort of my family room, but shortly after, during one of his weekend visits, Phil's sister asked if we would sing together at her church. Again, I agreed, so we took our repertoire of *one song* and shared it with that congregation.

I distinctly remember Phil being so kind and complimentary during our practice for that service. I was so uncomfortable singing in public. He encouraged me, although I'm not sure he was being totally truthful. Perhaps love is truly blind—*and* a little deaf as well.

From the beginning of our courtship, Phil was interested, not only in me, but in what I was doing musically. At the age of fourteen, I recorded the second of a three-album series, *Kimberly Keaton at the Keyboard, 2.* I received the following letter from Phil a few days before I went to the studio:

> Dear Kim,
> I'll be praying for you about this album. I'm very confident that the Lord is going to give you just the right songs that will minister to the hearts of people. You have a special gift there— that you can speak to the hearts of people with your piano music, not everyone has that ability. I'll be praying for you—especially on Thursday.

Over the next three years, our relationship blossomed, though not without some ebb and flow. I was so young, and our personalities were very different. Phil states he had never encountered a girl so reticent, so careful and guarded. He was sure about me from the beginning, but I kept my deepest feelings about him pretty close to my heart.

As usual, Phil was looking way down the road. He was going to marry me although he didn't share this with me then! I *was* smitten with him, and there was definite chemistry between the two of us, but my personality sometimes pushed back. Phil was never dissuaded, just a little bewildered at times.

I loved Phil's personality, so full of dreams, so directed, so confident, so optimistic. He personified the saying, "Go big or go home!" which both attracted and intimidated me at the same time. I received a second letter from Phil in the days leading up to my second recording. I was fifteen. When we rediscovered this recently, we both laughed at the way it clearly detailed the way Phil's mind has always worked.

> July 23, 1985
> Dear Kim,
> I imagine you've checked into Pinebrook, Bill Gaithers studio in Alexandria, IN? It would probably be very expensive though.

I would love to see you have a real orchestra on some of the songs that you play, but again, the cost is outrageous.

There was something else I've been thinking about. Did you ever think of trying to get your records distributed nationally?

If you could sign a contract with a distributing company—and I really think you could do it. I know it sounds far fetched but I really think that as good as your albums sound, you could do it.

I guess you need a manager. Are you looking for any volunteers?

I mentioned in an earlier chapter that I had performed some piano concerts as fundraisers for our school. The last of these took place on December 6, 1985, which was also the date of my seventeenth birthday.

Phil and I had discussed marriage, but when he exuberantly shared with me his plan to propose to me *on stage the night of the concert,* I was astonished and appalled! The thought of all that attention, directed at me—at us—was overwhelming. I felt myself recoiling inside. It was just too much for this self-conscious girl! *"Please* don't do that," I pleaded, dampening his spirits in a way I kind of regret today. I know and understand Phil so much better today, of course, and have learned to appreciate that this is just the kind of guy he is—over-the-top romantic who does everything with a flair, and to the *hilt!* Today, it is truly one of the things I love most about him, but at that time I couldn't imagine sharing such a private moment with so many people.

The concert proved to be a beautiful night, however, as Phil and I sang "White Christmas" together, and he presented me with a beautiful bouquet of white roses. The proposal would just have to wait.

One month later, on January 31, 1986, Phil took me on a walk through a beautiful park near my home. In the quiet of early evening, Phil asked me to become his wife. As we stood with only the barren trees and the cold winter sky listening in, I said "Yes." We ended the evening with a meal at a nearby Shoney's restaurant, where we lingered, savoring the joy, and dreaming of our future together.

Such simplicity was a far cry from the proposal Phil had envisioned—an elaborate display of his love and devotion with friends and family looking on. He was a bit puzzled at the time by my desire for privacy, but I think he finally decided that eliciting a firm "*Yes,*" and getting me to the altar, was *most* important. He'd figure the rest out later on.

In writing this book, we have enjoyed reading over my journals; journals filled with the details of the way things were in the beginning. We have laughed and psychoanalyzed ourselves and the way each of us roll. Did my childhood and teenage experiences of always being up front and visible contribute to my craving for privacy and solitude? Probably. My core personality, too, just longed to be the mouse in the corner. Phil saw in me so much potential, and has spent decades patiently, gently (and sometimes not so gently), coaxing the mouse in me out of the shadows. After thirty-four years of marriage, he knows me best and loves me still.

With the patience of Phil, a lot of maturing, and love of my Heavenly Father, I have come a long way. Just last year I turned fifty, and Phil, in his own words, "took a great risk" and surprised me with an amazing birthday party. I don't know how he pulled off dinner, an elaborate cake, a lighted grand piano ice sculpture, and 125 guests in our home without me having a clue, but he did. I was so touched. I understood how much time, energy, and planning he expended for me. It was a grand display of his love, and in my heart, I believe he was making up for the downplayed marriage proposal more than thirty years earlier. On this night, all the creative romance and flair came pouring out. And I absolutely relished every moment of that evening and the people who shared it with us.

Phil and I graduated in May of 1986, I from high school, and Phil from college, and I spent the summer traveling with a quartet and planning a wedding. Phil and I were very detailed about the ceremony, carefully choosing each song, scheduling rehearsals with the musicians, and really (although we didn't realize it at the time) just doing what we would do for the rest of our lives together: planning a mini production!

On September 26, 1986, we stood before God and 650 friends and family members, and spoke those infamous words—"I do." At the close of the nearly *two-hour* ceremony our family joined us on stage to sing the beautiful song written by Tim Shepherd, titled "As For Me and My House."

We had no way of knowing on that beautiful autumn evening just what "serving the Lord" would look like for our family, but we meant every word.

Although Phil and I knew we would someday be doing music ministry together, he had, for the immediate future, taken a managerial position at a commercial cleaning company. I was planning to pick up a few house cleaning jobs to help cover our expenses as well. This meant I would be primarily at home—like normal people! I couldn't wait! To be home for an extended period of time would be a slice of heaven after the nomadic nature of my teenage years.

We settled into marriage and had the time of our lives setting up our small apartment. This was where more of our differences emerged. I came from a family of nine children. My father was in full-time ministry. So, when Phil told me to go ahead and shop for curtains, I went to K-mart. I was so surprised when his response was, "K-Mart? You don't buy curtains at K-Mart!" I informed him that we (my family) *certainly* did so. He brought home a JCPenney catalog, and when I saw the prices I thought it was ridiculous to spend that much money on curtains. I bought baloney; he wanted Turkey Pastrami from the deli. I bought the black and white generic brand; he wanted the name brand, and on it went. To this day, I'm the frugal one, and it has come in handy many times, and actually saved our necks on occasion.

We hung those "expensive" curtains, and decorated our tiny one-bedroom space. I loved planning meals to cook for the two of us, although my culinary skills were *dreadful*. One evening I decided to make spaghetti and realized I didn't even know how to boil noodles. And when I attempted pancakes, and ended up with nothing but charred pieces of batter stuck to the pan, Phil sweetly offered to take me out to eat. I was relieved, and scraped the remnants of our dinner into the trash, resolving to deal with the burnt skillet later. If you would have told me I would someday publish a cookbook, I would have laughed out loud. I discovered, however, that I was very domestic and loved being at home. Phil and I took long walks each evening, and life fell into a routine that brings a smile to my face even now.

We didn't have a piano, and I missed it sorely. There were times my fingers would itch to play. I remember running my fingers along the ten keys on the miniature grand piano telephone we had received as a wedding gift. It actually played the notes, and I'd lightly play a scale when I felt desperate. I was ecstatic on the day Phil surprised me with a beautiful glossy white Samick studio piano as a gift for my eighteenth birthday. It took up nearly half of our tiny living room, but I would have gladly given up my couch to make room for it.

I didn't know it at the time, but six weeks into our marriage Phil was already asking the question, "God, did I spend all those years preparing for the calling you gave me at fourteen for this?" Phil was sensitive to my needing to be home for a bit, but was sitting on "go" and couldn't *imagine* spending much time in his current job. He felt a desperate need to hear from God, so without telling me, he prayed a simple prayer, "God if you indeed have music ministry in our future, please help someone to call me and ask us to sing this weekend!"

That very week, Phil received a call from a minister asking us to come and provide music at his church that weekend. Phil was *overjoyed*, but when he shared this news with me... I laid on our bed and cried, even though I hid my tears from Phil. I loved music, I loved sharing it with the world, and I loved working for the Lord. But I was a new bride, relishing my husband, the quiet days at home, and the newness of all things domestic, and I wasn't ready for it to be disrupted—not yet.

We couldn't have known then just how formative those early days and years would be for both of us. The path God would choose to take us down would be long and circuitous, but every bend and rough place along the way was necessary. God unhurriedly began working out his plan in our lives. As I finished growing up, and Phil and I grew together as a couple, we began to learn many important things about God, ourselves, and one another. Ever so slowly, God began to beautifully blend Phil's calling and my gift into something He would use for our good and His glory. And what a journey it has been!

5

TAKE A STEP OF FAITH

Take a step of faith, it's time to move;
Lay aside your fears, and watch what God will do.
There's victory ahead, that mountain's not too high;
Friend, hold on, cause you're about to climb.[2]

On a warm, May evening in 1999, Phil secured a babysitter and took me out for the evening. We landed at a Wendy's restaurant, about all our budget would allow in those days. Nevertheless, I was thrilled for a few moments of peace and a break from the noise and chaos of our four kiddos—all under the age of ten at the time. A hamburger and a frosty in a quiet space tasted as life-giving to me as filet mignon served on fine china. We ordered, and I found a seat while waiting for Phil to bring our food.

I watched as he made his way to our table with the brown, plastic tray. I was looking forward to an hour of "catching up" and uninterrupted conversation with him. As he sat the tray down and took his seat, he looked at me and said, "Kim, I have something to tell you." My pulse quickened. I knew that tone of voice! Whatever was coming, it was going to be significant. I quickly strengthened my resolve and thought to myself, *Bring it on, Phil!* I'd been from "Dan to Beersheba" with this man and was confident I could handle at least one more "adventure."

2 The Collingsworth Family, track # 8, *That Day is Coming*, Stowtown Records, 2015, CD

Phil and I had now been married thirteen years, and while we had traveled together *part-time as music ministers* for revivals, conferences, and church camps, Phil had built quite the resume for himself in other arenas as well. He had served as minister of music in two different churches, worked as Director of Music for a small Bible college, had been Regional Claims Manager at Metropolitan Life, and was currently serving as Dean of Enrollment Management for his alma mater in Cincinnati, Ohio. Life was busy. All four of our children, Brooklyn, Courtney, Phillip, and Olivia were born during these years, and we had owned four homes, a fifth wheel RV, and a motor home.

Phil and I have sometimes referred to these thirteen years as our "Wilderness Experience." Not because they were terrible, though, for they were not. These years were wonderful in so many ways, and God used each bend and turnaround to teach us important lessons. But they were "messy" years. And while we had kept the main things intact—love for God, love for one another, and love for our children— we had never found our niche—that sweet spot in ministry where we belonged; where we could spread our wings; where we could be who we were meant to be; where we could fulfill our calling; where we could expend the creative energy God had given us.

Before marriage, we each had developed connections during our years of traveling with our respective Bible colleges, connections which had led to various job offers in music ministry *after* we were married. Truth is, Phil was gifted not only in music, but in administration and management. And to each ministry position Phil accepted, he brought his usual flair and sense of alacrity and enthusiasm to the table. Every choir he directed was dynamic; every event he planned just a bit "out of the box." And though we have maintained good relationships with each of these ministries, he was told time and again, "Phil, it's too much!" or, "You're way over the top!" Some painful misunderstandings resulted, and over the course of those thirteen years I had heard countless times, "Kim, this just isn't me! I don't fit!" Eventually we had begun to realize that perhaps God had something different for us.

So, when Phil's next words to me were, "Kim, I've resigned from my job," I took a deep breath, and said, "Ok, what's next?"

I think Phil finally understood with clarity that he had been trying to fulfill his calling in ways God had not intended. Over and over again, he had attempted to fit a mold that was never meant for him. And in recent months, I had come to the conclusion that neither Phil nor I could ever be happy and fulfilled in ministry while playing roles *others* thought best for us, but roles we felt ill prepared to play. I had finally said to him in exasperation one day, "Phil, you just need to work for *yourself.*" I had *no* idea what that meant, but I said it anyway! He took me seriously.

Phil was weary of feeling frustrated, conflicted, and suppressed. Experience, maturity, and the Holy Spirit have helped us to know ourselves. Phil and I both tend to be fixers, and when one thing doesn't work, we immediately set about to figure out why, and look for ways to resolve the situation. We had maneuvered the "chess pieces" of our lives for thirteen years until God, in his steadfast love and providence, placed us in "checkmate." He positioned us in such a way, on *purpose,* to get our full attention, and to clearly mark a new path He would have us follow.

My "what's next?" query would be answered in the weeks following as we sought the Lord together. And then one day Phil said, "Kim, we are going to sing! I am called to music ministry with my family! I *know* this is what God wants." He continued, "We will begin by taking every date that comes in—no more side jobs for me—I'm all in! I'm finished with trying to work in the insurance field and sing on the side, work for a church and sing on the side, and pursuing any other job that requires *my calling* to take a backseat." I had never seen Phil more sure or resolute. I was tentative but resigned, on board but more than a little terrified.

Truth is, I had always known that Phil had a special calling on his life. I was reminded of this recently when I came across a letter which he wrote to me very early in our relationship. Phil was a nineteen-year-old sophomore in college, and I was barely fifteen when I received the following:

Dear Kim
November 8, 1983
The Missionary Convention ended up really good. Sunday
night they had a dedication service for all the young people to give
their lives to the Lord for full-time Christian work.
About ninety percent of the student body went forward. (I
went).
I don't think I've ever told you; but I have a call into music
evangelism.
I'm not quite sure where or how I'll do it. But I would love to
be in full-time music ministry somehow.
There are so many ways that music is used in services—I just
hope I will be able to have my desires fulfilled.
Phil

Phil and I *had* been making music together from our earliest days
as a married couple. We had sung our first revival meeting together just
six weeks into our marriage, but our music and traveling were always
worked around Phil's "other" jobs. I remember too well, before we had
children, packing Phil's supper, picking him up at his office (one hour
from our house), and him eating while we drove to wherever it was we
happened to be singing that night. I loved singing, and traveling was part
of my DNA too. It was what I knew. But, honestly, I also relished the safety and predictability of that "main job" Phil always maintained. That sure
and steady paycheck gave me a sense of security which I was reluctant
to release. We never knew what our pay would be when singing. And
sometimes the offerings were abundant, exceeding our needs, but then
other times…well, we pretty much sang for free.

When the kids came along, we integrated them into our ministry as
soon as they could speak. I recently found an interesting journal entry
from 1996. Brooklyn would have been seven and Courtney, five:

> We practiced some with the girls before church, and they sang to-
> night. They did so well. We're really working on their pitch prob-
> lems—it's coming.

In the early years, our summers were typically our most busy seasons of music ministry. Phil would sometimes quit his side job for the

summer so we could accept nine or ten extended length church camp opportunities. And these were often remarkable, meaningful days of ministry, but exhausting too. We would typically lead worship and sing for three services each day—morning, afternoon and evening. This was no small undertaking, especially with young children. Taking care of their persistent needs, getting to each service on time, and being mentally and spiritually prepared for ministry took its toll, and on at least one occasion clouded my judgment.

It was a Sunday evening and we were preparing for the very last service of Beulah Camp in Pennsylvania. Brooklyn and Courtney were almost five and three years old. I was *so* tired, they were tired, and we were planning to drive several hours toward home after the service ended. I decided to bathe the girls, put them in their pajamas, and just leave them in our little cabin during the service. Now, from where I sat in the large camp tabernacle, I knew that by looking out the open sides, I would have a perfect view of the cabin. I supplied the girls with coloring books, crayons, their dolls and toys, and plenty of snacks. As I instructed them to *stay* in the living room and play, they nodded their heads solemnly, *promising* to do as they were told.

During the service I kept my eye on the little cabin and things seemed to be going well—until about halfway through the service. I looked out and saw what looked very much like two little orphans standing on the front porch. They both looked a little distressed standing there in their pajamas, bare feet, and Courtney's hair in a wild frizzy halo about her head. Something also seemed off with the window and the curtains that I knew had been hanging there earlier that evening. I was mortified knowing that most of the audience had the same view I had. The camp speaker, Rev Butch Heath, sitting beside Phil leaned over and chuckled, whispering, "That's what you call 'camp tramps'!" I wasn't aware until later that Phil had been worriedly watching the "cabin scene" play out from the platform. He had witnessed the pull-down window blind moving up and down rapidly before it snapped and sent the whole window treatment crashing down. I hurried from the tabernacle over to the cabin to tend to the girls, and found the pile of curtains, blinds, and rod on the floor. It was obvious they had gotten a bit rowdy, and their traipsing out onto the porch wasn't as much *disobedience* as it was a desperate plea for help. I don't recall if I punished them or not, but looking back, I hope I was merciful!

I loved coming home after a busy summer of travel and ministry. I homeschooled the girls, and we lived on a schedule. I thrived on planning and organization, loved making menus, grocery shopping, cooking, decorating, and all things domestic. Nothing made me happier in those days than to be gifted a day out and $50 to peruse all the local Goodwill stores. And the treasures I found were amazing.

I love music, of course, and Phil declares that I belong to the "Musical Freak Club." I'm not sure this is always meant to be a compliment, but I think he means I won't rest or relent until the note or arrangement we're working on is *right!* Not almost right...*right!* But to be honest, I've had no big musical aspirations of my own; I've never dreamed of a big career! I do remember, as a young girl, dreaming about having my own studio someday (a dream that is now finally coming to fruition at fifty-one years of age), but that's been about the extent of my big goals. Though I am intense and perfectionistic when it comes to the *music,* I have never delved into the commercial and promotional side of our ministry. Phil has always been the one with the big ideas, dreams, and idealistic ways to improve and grow the CFAM. I was called to the music ministry because my husband was called. I'm rather old fashioned in that way. I was taught by my mother's example to follow and support my husband, to take care of my children and my home, and I'm content in this role. I see now that God knew just how much I needed Phil's drive and motivation to help me realize God's fuller plan and purpose for me!

We moved into the summer of 1999, and when Phil's job ended in June, we were officially on our own. We did have several church camps scheduled for the summer, and were grateful. As we moved into fall, we had a few conferences and revival meetings, but Phil was looking ahead with concern to December. Most churches do not schedule special meetings during December due to all the activities surrounding Christmas.

In the past, we had performed a few one-night Christmas programs during the month of December. During one of these early Christmas programs, we sang our first family harmony! I dressed Brooklyn up as Mary, and she came out on stage singing:

> Mary had a little Lamb,
> Little lamb, little lamb;
> Mary had a little lamb,
> Was born on Christmas Day

We made up the next verse on which Courtney took the lead and Brooklyn sang the harmony above her.

> Wise men saw his star one night,
> Star one night, star one night;
> Wise men saw his star one night,
> Far brighter than the rest.

And then the girls and I sang three parts as they went into,

> They followed it to where Jesus lay,
> Jesus lay, Jesus lay;
> They followed it to where Jesus lay,
> And bowed to worship him.

> He died upon the cross one day,
> Cross one day, cross one day;
> He died upon the cross one day,
> He cared that much for me

And then we took it up a half step as Phil and I came in singing harmony while the girls carried the melody,

And He washes all our sins away,

Sins away, sins away;

He washes all our sins away

In Calvary's Crimson flow.[3]

It was simple, but God's presence would come, and the tears would flow as the pure Gospel was delivered through song. Phil and I were thrilled to be integrating the children into the music.

We began receiving calls from pastors inquiring about the Christmas concerts. We scheduled eight or ten of these one-night programs in December of 1999. We worked very hard to make them memorable. Some may remember the birthday cake we brought for Jesus each night and how five-year-old Phillip carried it down the aisle singing:

Happy birthday, Jesus,[4]

I'm so glad it's Christmas;

All the tinsel and lights

And the presents are nice,

But the real gift is you.

Happy birthday, Jesus,

I'm so glad it's Christmas;

All the carols and bells

Make the holiday swell,

But it's all about you.

Happy Birthday, Jesus,

Jesus, I love you

We actually used a real chocolate cake a few times but wisened up when the kids couldn't resist dipping their fingers in for a taste. I had someone make us one from plaster—much less irresistible!

3 The Collingsworth Family, written by Kim to the tune of Mary Had a Little Lamb, live concert events
4 The Brooklyn Tabernacle Choir, *Happy Birthday Jesus*, Oh, What A Love, Warner Chappel Music, Inc, Sony/ATV Music Publishing LLC, 1992. Written by Carol Cymbala

Those Christmas concerts opened a brand-new door for our family. We began to get inquiries from pastors wondering if we would be willing to conduct a one-night gospel concert at their church, a new concept for us, but one that just felt "right." This paradigm shift from conferences, camps, and revival services, to gospel concert events was exciting, and we knew God was opening new doors for our family.

Phil and I prayerfully decided to officially launch a new phase of ministry on January 1, 2000. We would pursue a *full-time* concert ministry, phasing out the conferences, revivals and church camps over the following months. We knew things were changing, and that our future ministry would look different. Had I known some of the obstacles we would face, I'm not sure I would have had the courage to take that step, but we have learned through experience that God doesn't always show us the clear path forward. Many times He just says, "Go—trust me." And when God calls and we obey, *He* assumes responsibility for us.

The test of "us"

One of the first tests we faced in this step of faith was...*us*! I wasn't quite prepared for how this new adventure would accentuate Phil's and my differences. Sure, we had been married for thirteen years, and I thought I knew my husband well. But as we launched out into the "deep end" of a new ministry, Phil was in a speed boat, moving ahead open throttle, while I lagged behind wading along the shore. Especially when it comes to life-changing decisions, I tend to be a cautious, pragmatic person who favors security and sure-footedness. I am a "bean counter." Phil on the other hand is full of titanic-sized dreams. He isn't afraid of risks and loves the thrill of sailing in uncharted waters. We laugh about it today, but when Phil presented the dream, my first question was always, "What's the plan?" This used to frustrate him to no end, because often he hadn't gotten to the planning phase! I was famous for quoting every Proverb I could remember that described the actions of the "prudent" (careful) person, and we probably could have sold tickets to some of those moments of "intense fellowship"—ok *fights*—we used to have!

Through launching a new ministry, we have discovered that Phil's visionary personality and my managerial gifts complement each other. But conversely, when I, the manager, refuse to get on the same page with Phil the visionary, I drain the dreams, the life, and the inspiration right out of him. I know this too well.

Truth is, God has spoken powerfully to me regarding our differences and my constant push back in the early days. I don't believe he wanted me to stop contributing my insights—Phil and I are a team. And as our friend Bill Gaither often said to the Homecoming artists just before we walked out on stage, "We're better together." I won't forget the day God whispered, "Kim, you are married to a visionary! You can either get on board and have a great adventure, or you can keep resisting and be miserable, because Phil is *never* going to stop dreaming." The truth of those words shifted something within me. And I made a decision to buckle my seatbelt and enjoy the ride! I've had to go back, remember, and embrace that truth countless times since. And I'll admit, I've not always gotten it right.

The test of trust

Another test in those early days was the test of trust. I'm not a big risk taker, and this step of faith God was asking us to take would require a measure of risk we *almost* didn't take. As we were launching our new ministry in early 2000, Phil decided we would make a professional studio recording. I was panic-stricken. I had a little PTSD from the one recording we had made ten years earlier, remembering it had cost us $5,000, and had taken four years to pay for. Selling cassette tapes at churches and camps at $5 each wasn't lucrative, especially when I'd often need to use the few dollars we'd make from sales for diapers or other necessities. But Phil was persuasive, and we began work on the project.

This would not be another duet album. The kids were singing with us regularly now, and we wanted to include them on this recording. On this album we would record some of our very first family songs, such as, "He's Always On Time," "All God's Children," and others. There were also three ballads (a poem or song narrating a story) on the album that we felt were too musically and lyrically mature for ten-year-old Brooklyn, so my sister Becky agreed to record with us.

Recording this album was an enormous leap of faith for Phil and me. We had a few concerts scheduled, and a few lingering revivals and church camps, but not nearly enough to take on such a financial responsibility. In March of 2000, we were scheduled to travel to North Carolina and meet with well-known gospel music producer, Roger Talley, to lay down the tracks. We had yet to meet him. My mom had flown in from Florida, and would be spending a few days with the children. Phil was exuberant, as usual, but on the eve of our trip I panicked and nearly backed out.

As we prepared for bed that night I was overwhelmed with doubts. I began giving voice to them. "Phil, we are so proud!" I remember saying. "Who do we think we are? No one will ever buy these CD's. We are presuming upon God." As I spoke, I witnessed something so dreadful that it makes me wince even now. I saw the hope and excitement drain from my husband's face. He was deflated and defeated, and Satan had used *me* *to* discourage him—so much so that he finally agreed with me. "Maybe you're right," he said, "I think I'm going to cancel!" With that, Phil called and left Roger a voicemail canceling our session for the following day.

I went to bed, and Phil went downstairs where he paced the floor praying until 3 a.m. I awakened early, and Phil lay beside me already awake. I'm not sure if he had slept at all. "How do you feel?" he asked. I replied, "Phil, I think Satan was fighting me last night." Phil was out of bed in a flash with a determined, "Kim, I feel the same. Get up, we are going to North Carolina!" He called and left Roger a second voicemail, "canceling" our cancellation! We got up early and left the house with mom and the children still sleeping. My mother never knew of our middle of the night turmoil.

From today's vantage point of twenty years, twenty-eight CDs, and sixteen DVDs, I understand this is typical, but we were novices then. Experience has taught us to intentionally fortify ourselves through prayer and fasting for the spiritual attacks we'll almost certainly face, especially when commencing something new. We have discovered that Satan hates the proclamation of the Gospel, even through music, and will stop at nothing to silence it if he can!

A few weeks after laying down the tracks on our new album, we traveled back to North Carolina with the children and my sister for the recording of our vocals. It was exciting, and the kids were all in, not even complaining about the long hours spent in the studio or singing the same lines over and over. I'll never forget six-year-old Phillip, after I'd just re-sung a line, winking at me and saying, "Good job, Mom," in the best "big-man" voice he could muster. He soaked up every minute of our first studio experience and was mesmerized by all of it— the microphones, the sound board, the tiny slides and blinking lights. Not surprisingly, that once little boy is busy building his own studio today.

By God's grace, and responsible budgeting, we paid for that recording a mere five and a half months following its release. What a miracle!

The test of finances

We continued moving forward in our vision for concert ministry, and little by little invitations came in. We weren't overwhelmed or besieged with requests, of course, and finances were scarce in those early days. In a journal entry from June, 2000, I wrote:

> We had a difficult month and had a $1,300-dollar deficit again this month—pretty scary. I'm not sure what the Lord is saying to us, but I'm willing to listen.

Another entry in those early months read:

Phil and I were up until almost 1 a.m. talking. He tells me that we're going to close the month out in the red again! God help us!

I'm puzzled by it all—it seems that God is blessing our product sales incredibly and he's helping us and the children with our music—but with travel expenses—our house payment etc.—it just seems like we can't make it on the road.

And another:

To bed approximately 12 a.m. after checking our email and website. There were three invitations in the email for concerts and one on the voicemail. It's unreal how God is opening the doors. Phil said to me tonight, "I'm going to keep having our prayer meetings—and let God do the rest.

The test of motive

A test every servant of Christ faces in ministry is the test of motives. We faced this test too.

In the midst of these uncertainties, we were certain we were doing what God had called us to do, and He was so gracious to give us landmarks along the way proving His faithfulness to His promises.

In those early days of the CFAM ministry, we were invited to sing for a minister's Christmas banquet in Alabama. We would be providing a full concert for the evening. After arriving at the venue to set up for the concert, the contact person who invited us informed Phil that they would *not* be giving us an honorarium. He went on to explain that our honorarium, instead, would be the "exposure" this event would give our family, thereby opening other potential concert opportunities in the future. We were less than impressed with this arrangement, to say the least. We were striving to live carefully and to budget according to approximated offering projections each month. We did not charge a fee but depended on the fairness and generosity of people. And as I once heard someone say, "You can't eat a 'God Bless You'!" Upon Phil's return to the motel, he shared this news with me. I can still remember Phil and me praying together and making a *conscious decision* that this event would be our love-offering to God.

At the minister's banquet we sang to a room full of wonderful pastors and their wives. God helped us, and we gave it *everything* we had, knowing that this night was on us—the gas, the food, the travel expense—all of it. It was *our* offering. As we packed up our sound equipment later that evening, the caterer for the event approached Phil and thanked him for the music. She expressed how much it had meant to her, and with that she thrust something into his hand and walked away. We were astonished to find she had given a very generous check. I would write in my journal that week,

> I've been thinking this week of how God takes care of us!

He sure does!

There were other dynamics I wrestled with as we launched this new ministry.

The test of whom will I fear

I grew up within a very conservative fellowship of churches. I had been playing piano and doing ministry in this particular church world since childhood. Phil shared the same background, so for the first thirteen years of our marriage and ministry we had worked primarily within this church culture. *These* were *our* people. They loved *us*, we loved *them*. They *encouraged* us, were *proud* of us, and used us in their churches, at their conventions, their colleges, and church camps. As God began to move us out into the broader church world, and thus into other denominations, while most of our friends were supportive, there were *many* who did not understand. Our non-sectarian approach was seen by some as a betrayal of sorts—a betrayal of our upbringing, our heritage, our roots. We were admonished to "Be careful." We were warned, "You're gonna lose your kids." And I'll never forget how one dear lady expressed her disappointment in us. Her exact words: "Our young people are watching you, and you're singing to…*them*."

Phil didn't struggle with this in the least. His response was simply, "Kim, Jesus died for everyone!" and he was right.

Phil was excited to begin using our new orchestrated tracks. He was always pushing ahead, desiring to update, improve, and evolve. And while I loved the progression of our music, I still worried about people's perception of us. If it was a concert setting, it was fine. But in the churches we grew up in, tracks weren't really used in worship. It just wasn't done. As we finished out our revivals and camp meetings, I'd beg Phil not to make me use a track to play the offertory, but he would turn it on anyway, and I'd be stuck. I would have happily laid aside our new music and sung the older and more traditional selections in these settings. Not Phil! He was going to sing the most current music we had recorded. I would write in my journal:

> April 5, 2000 —I'm struggling a little bit with transition—in the fact that I don't want to be a nuisance in the revival meetings with our music. I pray that God helps us to be very sensitive to what's appropriate and what is not. God, please help us to sing only what you want us to sing.

And again:

> I'm struggling to figure out how to be appropriate in a revival setting with concert style music (tracks etc.).
> God is helping us—I'm praying for a fresh anointing of God on our music—Would you help us, God, to be anointed with your presence—that people don't see us—but you.

This was truly the cry of my heart.

I am a pleaser. I am a person who enjoys making other people happy—and this means I didn't want to make anyone *unhappy*. And honestly, these interactions with people whom I loved, respected, and had been playing piano for my whole life were very painful. But God used the pain to drive me to my knees and to show me some things I needed to see.

I began to see that for many years I had lived to please God—*and* man—instead of God *alone*. I was committed to God and His plan for me, but also very committed to man—how people thought I should dress, act, or react.

I realize now that by constantly "pushing back" when Phil wanted to expand or try something new and different in our ministry, I was actually putting *my* limitations on God. *I* was dictating how He could work in our lives and ministry. My silent motto was, "If my peers disdain it, don't consult God; I already know the answer."

The bondage I felt was miserable. I was often resisting Phil—and not because of God, but because of the fear of man. The wisdom of God's Word is so true when it admonishes, "*The fear of man brings a snare, but whoever trusts in the Lord shall be safe*" *(Proverbs 29:25 NKJV).*

Phil had a way of seeing things more clearly than I did at times. He was following God's call, and I needed to follow him. It was a process—dying to myself and everyone else, and following my husband and God.

I won't forget falling on my face before the Lord and telling Him, "It's okay God. I just want you to use me in whatever way you desire. Here's my gift. Here's everything we have—everything we own—it's all yours."

I am so thankful for the encouragers in our life during those early days. Phil's mom and my parents were our biggest cheerleaders. My father, a leader in our church world, always defended us against criticism, and never failed to share a word from the Lord with us. When I lamented on occasion of the tough spots we were in, he'd say, "Kim, God takes care of His own!" Even in the midst of opposition, there were still those who believed in us and in what we were doing. God used one man in particular to bolster our courage during a tough time.

We were invited to Salem, Ohio to sing for a Christmas banquet hosted by a local church. The pastor was truly a great man—a giant in our church world. He had watched both Phil and me grow up. I had played piano in places where he was speaking from the time I was a child. He was getting on in years now, but was still a passionate speaker, a lover of God's Word, and a "big C" church guy.

After the crowd had gone, and we were preparing to pack up our equipment, Dr. Harold Schmul stayed behind to chat with us. As we talked, I sat on the front row while he straddled the altar facing Phil, who sat opposite him. He complimented us on our music and ministry, and then said, "Phil, there are some in our church world who think you're too professional. But I do not. You go where God calls you." And his final word: "Court them all, but don't marry any of them!" We knew what he meant. We were called to serve the whole body of Christ and not allow denominational lines, subcultures, and barriers to restrict us from following the Lord's leading. That loving affirmation from one whom both Phil and I respected so much was a blessing from the Lord and gave us the direction and courage we desperately needed.

During those fledgling years of the CFAM ministry, I was often reminded of the admonition given me by my father years before. I was going through a tough time when I received a letter from him. "Kimberly," he admonished, "Life is like a train ride through a beautiful countryside. It's not about the destination or making the next depot on time; it's about enjoying the view from whatever vantage point God has placed you. Sit back and enjoy the journey! If you'll stay in your seat and focus on what is right before you, you will begin to witness the breathtaking wonder of God's grace and goodness juxtaposing the darkness and difficulty." It was a timely word for me, and I suspect for some of you as well.

Our family's step of faith into the unknown was the beginning of a journey that continues today. And though the ride has been sometimes fraught with challenges, I have marveled at the ways we've witnessed God's care and the wide-open doors He's given us. We've only had to *stay in our seats*! We haven't yet reached our destination, but it's not about that. My heart still resonates with what I wrote at the end of that most difficult year:

> I know that the devil hates what we're doing, but we're not quitting! We have found our niche in life!

I don't know what the journey looks like from your window on the train, but if I could offer any encouragement it would simply be this: When God calls you, take that step of faith and never quit. For one called by God, quitting is never an option. Though the ride may get rough, *stay in your seat!*

6

TUESDAY EVENING PRAYERS

Prayer is the mightiest agent to advance God's work.
—E.M. Bounds

Earlier this week, after our grown children had gone home and the house was quiet, I slipped into the piano room to relax and unwind. It had been a busy day—the kids had been in and out, and the tell-tale signs the grandkids had enjoyed their day at "Nana's" were still scattered about. I sat at the piano and began to play, feeling my shoulders relax as the music, arranged against the backdrop of stillness, began to soothe the taut strands of busyness. I've always loved this time of day, these serene moments when my creative juices flow and I find the artist in me most productive.

My quiet oasis was interrupted by Phil, calling from the other room, "Kim, are you ready to pray?" I paused the music and answered, "I'm ready." It was Tuesday night…It was time to pray.

I was greatly impacted by the book, *Fresh Wind, Fresh Fire*, by Pastor Jim Cymbala, in the early days of the CFAM ministry, and God used it in a powerful way to tune my mind toward Him. His emphasis on prayer and the stories of transformation *through* prayer made me hungry for a spirit of prayer in my own life.

On January 22, 2000, I sat on the piano bench at Calvary Church of the Nazarene in Columbus, Indiana. The children had finished singing and exited the platform to take their seats on the front row. I watched them and continued playing softly as Phil introduced our next song. They were growing up. Brooklyn, ten, was finding her singing voice— one which hinted already at being dynamic and strong. Courtney was only eight, but she had a way of keeping us "real" with her forthright opinions and the ability to see and vocalize the 'funny" in just about every situation. Phillip, at five, was wide-eyed and interested in all the trappings of setting up sound. He was beginning to learn how to wrap cords, and took it *very* seriously. I glanced at Olivia. She was occupied with the contents of her book bag, her little red head down. The thick glasses she wore (which often slid down the bridge of her tiny nose) gave her a "wise old soul" look that belied the fact she was not yet two.

I don't recall the song I played that night, but I will never forget the gentle voice of the Holy Spirit as he began to speak to me. The weight of my responsibility to these kiddos settled down upon me. I felt God say to me, *"There is so much I could do through your little family...but you're so busy—you don't pray."*

I had been a follower of Jesus since childhood—I prayed and read my Bible nearly every day. But I felt God calling me to something deeper, a prayer life that was more intentional—more fervent and consistent. God continued speaking, and I continued playing, but my heart and mind were in another place. And as I listened, He gave me this clear but simple mandate: First, I want you to pray that those four children sitting on the front seat will come to know Me. I want you to understand that no matter where you travel or how much you sing, your first responsibility is to them. Second, I want you to pray that your family will be effective out here for My Kingdom—not yours. The only way your ministry is going to touch people and have a powerful, lasting impact, is through prayer.

As we traveled home that evening, I was so deeply stirred by God's message to me that I shared it with Phil. We decided while driving home that night, that in addition to our personal prayer times we would begin by setting aside a designated time on Tuesday evenings for prayer. We would pray together.

According to a Family Life survey, Phil and I were like 94% of other Christian couples. We had never intentionally prayed together. We enjoyed devotions most evenings with our children. We taught them God's Word, and we prayed with *them*, but to kneel *together* as a couple and lay our praise and petitions before God—this was something altogether new. I must admit it felt awkward and uncomfortable on that first Tuesday evening. We sat together for a while, and with pen and paper made a list of our prayer priorities. And when we knelt, we didn't fully understand that we were in fact, laying the cornerstone for our marriage, our family, and for the CFAM ministry.

I wrote in my journal the following day:

> Last night—it was wonderful. Our prayer requests were (among others):
> 1. Our four children
> 2. That God would anoint our singing and playing in an unusual way
> 3. His leadership in our music ministry and the transition from the revival/camp meeting circuit to more of a concert ministry.
>
> I believe the devil hates it when we pray, and he fights it every time. I know one thing for sure though: God will honor our prayers!

For me, this chapter is the most important chapter in this book, because I came to understand that without *constant, consistent prayer,* our family could not have persevered in this ministry God had called us to. Without prayer, our Christian service would be hollow. Without prayer, our spiritual *gifts* would not flow out of a life of love.

God knows I am simple. He gave me a simple mandate for how we should pray. As our ministry grew and expanded, so did our prayer life. God wanted to do so much more in our personal lives to form us into the image of Jesus. In the place of prayer, he had our attention. Reflecting over twenty years and reading through dozens of journals, it's evident that prayer has been the key; prayer has pulled us through incredibly tough times and kept us on the right path.

Prayer has preserved our marriage

Most people know that working together all day—*every day*—is difficult at best for any marriage. As Phil and I *together* leaned into the effort it would take to grow and expand the CFAM ministry, we were no different from other couples. During the first years, finances were tight, we lived on a budget down to the penny, and still barely kept our heads above water. Our different personalities only added to the stress. There were times on Tuesday nights that I really didn't want to be in the same room with this man, much less pray with him. Our commitment to the Lord alone kept us on our knees. We discovered something wonderful. We found that it's impossible to pray with someone when you feel anger or irritation with that person. We were committed to pray, and this commitment caused us to sit together when things were tough, communicate authentically, forgive one another, and only then could we really talk to our Heavenly Father. God used these difficult times to humble us, to show us our selfish ways—our insensitivities—and to drive us to repentance before God and one another.

We also learned that when we couldn't come to an agreement on a matter, often God would use prayer to change one of our minds, align us with the other, and bring resolution.

We were so grateful when our first project as a family was successful. We had the idea to do a three-part piano project. "Sunday Morning Ivories" would be a two-part worshipful medley of praise songs and hymns. We would also record "Silver and Ivory," which would be a piano and trumpet project. Our first recording was selling well, the ministry was progressing, and Phil, with his typical gusto, wanted to do all three of these new projects at the same time. The sun was shining and people were buying our recordings, so why not produce *all three at once*?

I was dying! The effort to prepare, arrange, and execute these projects, in addition to being a wife and homeschooling mom was impossible for me. Phil was adamant that we should push through. We couldn't agree, and duking it out in the flesh was *not* working for either of us. I remember the night we went to prayer. I knelt, and Phil paced the floor. We got quiet, just listening to the Lord. After some time, Phil knelt beside me and said without a hint of resentment, "Kim, you're right, it's too much." Hindsight has proved the wisdom of God. To forge ahead with all three projects would have been financially, and physically devastating.

There were times when these prayer meetings just got us in the same room, which led to needed conversations. One of my journal entries details this:

> Today has been extremely rough—for some reason I have felt down and depressed—I was set for our prayer meeting, but we ended up talking the entire time. It was very profitable and needed. Our marriage was needing some TLC and we spent two hours hashing things out. Our ministry has gotten so busy that we've allowed our marriage to suffer—both of us feel so much better about everything.

These times have a way, still today, of bringing us together, aligning our priorities, helping us recognize when we are too busy, and forcing us to find solutions that work.

As our ministry began to grow, I would write:

> January 22, 2002
> I just pray that God helps us to stay on the right track and help these prayer meetings to remain the central focus of our ministry. This is our key to a powerful anointed ministry. Please God, let it be so.

Prayer has aligned our priorities

While reading through my journals, I noticed that at around six years into this ministry things became a little bumpy. I see now that this was a time when our ministry was beginning to soar. There were amazing things happening, awesome opportunities were coming our way, and it was both wonderful and frightening all at the same time. We reached a new phase of "busy" we hadn't known. Phil was occupied night and day just keeping up with the promotional and business side of the CFAM. I was raising four children, homeschooling, arranging music, and conducting rehearsals. During this season our prayer times continually drove us back to the basics. Through prayer God gently drew us back to the all-important center: God first, our marriage, our children, and *then* ministry. We had to make conscious decisions to stay focused on the most important matters at hand. As our children moved into their teenage years, and as their needs shifted, we had to keep adjusting and restructuring so as to not threaten these most important God-given priorities.

As the requests for concerts poured in, we realized that while this was a blessing from the Lord, we must pull back and draw clear boundaries in order to prevent our family life from descending into chaos. I'm sure there are others who can perhaps manage more than I, but I thrive on structure, and when things feel overwhelming or out of control, I shut down.

I remember a conversation when Phil looked at me incredulously and stated, "Kim, this is a great date, we *can't* turn this down!" "Yes we can, because I can't get the kids homeschooling done if we take that date," I replied. The schedule threatened to be all-consuming and a source of conflict. God continually worked on *both* of us in this matter. In 2007 I would reflect on this in my journal:

> I've been asking God to give me a quiet spirit and discretion in all things—I need to hold my opinions to myself when it comes to Phil (schedule). God is helping me—change my heart God. My prayer is this: "Create in me a clean heart, O God; and renew a right spirit within me. Cast me not away from your presence; and take not thy Holy Spirit from me. Restore unto me the joy of thy salvation, and renew a right spirit within me" (Psalm 51:10-12 KJV).

It was through prayer that God showed us a path—one that worked for all of us. We came to the following resolutions: I would have jurisdiction over Monday through Thursday. This portion of the week was mine. We would not travel or sing on these days. This would allow me to focus on the kids, the home, the schooling, and the music during the week. Our children could attend functions at a nearby Christian school, be involved in team sports, and attend VBS. We could go as a family to our home church on Sunday, attend Boone County Fair (and other community events), and our children could grow up with some structure and "normalcy." We would sing no more than nine dates a month.

I recall sitting across the table from our booking agent as he pleaded with us to acquiesce on this decision. It was tough. He complained that churches and promoters sometimes didn't understand when he turned down a date. But when he started explaining to those same wonderful pastors and promoters the "why" of our decision, he found that people were gracious and kind.

Our nine monthly concert dates were scheduled over three weekends, giving us one weekend each month to be home. I guarded these weekends tenaciously, earning me the nickname, "Mamma Kim," by our booking agent and others. I wear the name proudly!

These decisions, made prayerfully, brought peace. Once these boundaries were set in stone, I was able to catch my breath and structure my life around them. There were times when we made exceptions, of course, but not without discussion and thought. Today, we perform ten concert dates each month, and anything more we put to a vote before our entire team.

Prayer has induced us to wait on the Lord for provision

On our very first family album, we recorded a song that quickly became our favorite. We were living the lyrics of this song titled, "He's Always on Time." The chorus went like this:

He's always on time I know,
Always on time.
You may be down to the wire,
Near the deadline;
And if your back is to the wall,
He'll be right there
When on him you call.
He's never too early,
But he's never late;
He's always on time.[5]

It was incredible to sit back and watch God provide for the needs of our growing ministry in those early days. Phil and I knew what it meant to suffer the consequences of *not* waiting on the Lord. We had known the sting that resulted from rushing ahead and answering our own prayers. We determined that with God's help we weren't going down that road again.

When we were faced with a need, we took it to prayer. There were times when God answered before we even asked. One Sunday morning, during our concert, our sound board made a thunderous noise, and then went silent. From the piano bench my mind was racing with "what are we going to do?" I knew just how expensive it would be to replace it, and I also knew we didn't have the money to do so. By the end of the day, we had received a check for the amount we needed to purchase a new one. We thanked God on our way home that weekend.

I remember a cold, blustery Sunday evening that found us in a small church in Indiana. The platform was tiny, and our outdated microphones with their "spaghetti bowl" of cords were a death trap for the kids. Later that week I journaled the following:

> God Is Faithful! I just love how He is always on time. Sunday night
> a man came to Phil and said the Holy Spirit had spoken to him

---

5 The Collingsworth Family, *He's Always on Time*, track #6, Lifting Our Voices, P&KC Music, 2000, CD

and told him to buy us new cordless mics. We've been blown away. God is teaching us to be quiet and just wait on Him.

And another reads:

We had a concert Thursday evening in Wilmot, Ohio, at the Amish Door Restaurant. A man came up to Phil, (Roger Stearns), asking questions about the girls' violins. He owns a music shop where he makes violins, violas, and cellos. He asked if we would come to his shop on Saturday. We did, and he gave the girls brand new violins. We were beside ourselves. The girls were thrilled. It's amazing how the Lord takes care of us on the road.

As we continued to book concerts and travel the country, it became increasingly difficult packing six of us in a van—with all our equipment. God had miraculously provided a lovely trailer that we pulled behind. I could actually iron our dress clothes ahead of time and hang them up! It was a blessing but still far from ideal. When traveling at night, we'd put the van seats down and make beds for the kids on the floor. I spent many long days sitting in the back with the kids, listening to Olivia read, drilling math facts and phonics with flashcards, or helping someone with their fractions. We didn't eat out much in those days, so I packed a cooler with food and passed paper plates with sandwiches over the seats to the children countless times as we rolled down the highway.

We tentatively began to pray for a bus. It seemed impossible! How could we ever afford what *seemed* like a luxury? Nevertheless, we took it to prayer. We trusted our Heavenly Father, and knew that if *He* deemed it necessary, *He* would provide the CFAM with a bus. I found several journal entries that detail my feelings about the matter, and my brutal honesty makes me smile today:

July 20, 2003
This has been a horrible day for me: My feet are swollen. I have been very grouchy, and I feel bad about it. But it's a bad combo to be in an SUV Excursion for thirteen hours with five other people. Oh Lord, in your time—please send us a bus! We need one so badly!

And on January 22, of 2004, I wrote:

> The kids have traveled well today. It seems they have argued a bit
> more. I think they're just a little frustrated. If God sees fit to give
> us a bus, I'll sure be happy, but only if it's His will. Otherwise, I'll
> just keep staying in hotels.

My faith had begun to rise a bit more when I wrote:

> Feb 16, 2004
> I'm praying a lot about a bus and just waiting on God to an-
> swer prayer, IF it is His will and in His good time. I love letting
> God do the driving. It is truly comfortable.

Some time later, we arrived in Columbia, Missouri, for an evening
concert. I had been ill for some weeks, and had just left the hospital earlier that week after having had a blood transfusion. I sat on the front
row with the children seated on either side of me while we waited to be
introduced. My legs felt leaden, and I wondered if I could walk up the
few stairs to the stage. *God, I don't have an ounce of strength to sing or
play tonight. Will you please strengthen me? I can't do this without your
help,* I prayed.

Somehow I made it to the piano. As we began, I can't explain what
happened. God came down and filled my whole being with the joy of the
Lord. I was infused with His presence and a strength that was supernat-
ural. But it is mostly the joy I remember. I stood to speak, and for three
or four minutes felt impressed to simply give praise to the Lord for His
goodness. God blessed that place with His sweet presence, and people
began to weep and give God praise. It was a wonderful evening.

There is a passage of scripture in Nehemiah 8:10, where Ezra in-
structs the downtrodden people of Israel who were weeping to rejoice,
because, "The joy of the Lord is your strength." This was immeasurably
true in my life on that night. In my weakness I had asked the Lord
to give me strength, and He gave me joy—joy which infused me with
strength.

Kim – age 3 (the age when she prayed for a gift)

Kim - age 6 (the age she played her first piano solo in church)

Kim's entire Family – James & Carolyn Keaton and their 9 children (Kim was 9 yrs of age here)

ABOVE: Kim playing piano at Stone City Christian Academy, Bedford, IN – Age 12
RIGHT: The first Union Bible College quartet Kim accompanied – Age 13
BELOW: Kim – Age 17, High School Graduation w/her father and older brother, Jeff

LEFT: Phil – Age 3
BELOW: Phil – Age 4, with his mother,
Billie Collingsworth and his two sisters,
Connie & Rena
BOTTOM: Phil – Age 16, with his father,
Raymond Collingsworth

ABOVE: *Phil's High School Graduation – Age 17,*
with his parents, Raymond & Billie Collingsworth
RIGHT: *Phil – Age 19, a special photo taken just*
for me
BELOW: *Phil – Age 21, Playing the organ in*
chapel at college

ABOVE: Our wedding day! September 26, 1986 BOTTOM LEFT: Kim – Age 17
I've always been up for a party! I had been married just 5 weeks here and what a
surprise for Phil when he saw his new bride dressed up like Pippi Longstocking.
BOTTOM RIGHT: Kim - Age 20 - Leaving the hospital with our first child, Brooklyn
Rose

LEFT: Our 4 children, just 5 months before our concert ministry began – Brooklyn (10), Courtney (8), Phillip (5), Olivia (15 months)

BELOW: A typical scene on the front row while I was playing a piano solo - Courtney & Phillip both asleep. Those were the days!

BOTTOM: The Collingsworth Family's first time in the studio together

Our first rig !!

LEFT: Our first bus – BIG RED! What an answer to prayer this was!

BELOW: Our 2nd Bus – Black Pearl

ABOVE: Olivia – Age 5

LEFT: Courtney – One of many days spent in the studio

BELOW: Phillip & Brooklyn – studio days. Always seeing the fun side of life

ABOVE: Backstage comic relief – A very common scene, back in the day

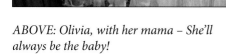

ABOVE: Olivia, with her mama – She'll always be the baby!

RIGHT: Phillip – A forever Cincinnati Reds fan, and proud of it!

Our 4 kids ready to sing at GaitherFest, Myrtle Beach

Courtney – Time for sports at Appalachian Youth Camp

BELOW: Olivia – with soldiers in Kosovo

The Collingsworth Family in Kosovo with General Jerry G Beck

The Collingsworth Family performing the CHRISTMAS IN KOSOVO video

The Collingsworth Family – moments before walking on stage at Music Hall, Cincinnati, OH

ABOVE: *The audience at Cincinnati's Historic Music Hall*

LEFT: *Phil & Kim with Uncle Charlie VanDemeer of Children's Bible Hour*

BELOW: *Everyone doing their part to get the orders out – It was a family affair*

*ABOVE: Just a day in the life of home schooling
RIGHT: This picture represents the end of a 19
year home schooling journey. Let the celebration
begin!
BELOW: Upon the completion of home schooling,
my four kids surprised me with flowers, beautiful
accolades, and a plaque in front of an audience in
North Carolina. A moment I will always cherish!*

Phillip's senior year – His final game with his basketball team … and yes, they WON!!

RIGHT: Yes, I really did drive the bus. And, yes ….. this happened while I was driving.

BELOW: Christmas Eve caroling with the family at Christ Hospital, Cincinnati, Ohio

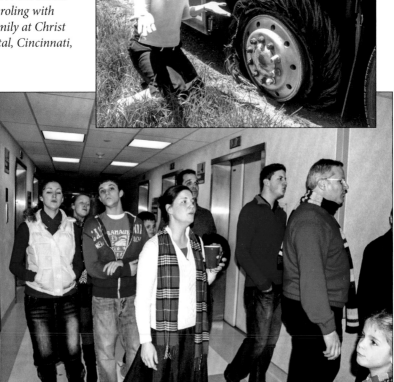

*RIGHT: Walking this road together
and enjoying the journey!
BELOW: 2008 – Singing for Bill &
Gloria Gaither's company Christmas
party
BOTTOM: Rehearsing with Dino
Kartsonakis for Parade of Pianos at
National Quartet Convention*

Phil & I, along with Dino & Cheryl Kartsonakis - getting ready to perform at the PARADE OF PIANOS at National Quartet Convention

ABOVE: Rehearsal with Lari Goss and Dino Kartsonakis in preparation for THE GRAND PIANO EXTRAVAGANZA

RIGHT: Surprise anniversary celebration from our four kids

ABOVE: 2009 Christmas getaway to Dollywood with the family

RIGHT: Date night with my favorite guy

BELOW: One of the many radio interviews we've done over the years - Daniel Britt/JOY FM

RIGHT: My dear friend, Janan Miller – her piano skills had a big impact on me as a child

BELOW: Both Brooklyn & Courtney found their wedding dresses on the same day. They were married less than 6 months apart.

BOTTOM: The CFAM doing what we love most - 2012

ABOVE: 2010 – Live video recording

RIGHT: With my friend, Joyce Bunch – the lady who played the bass guitar with me on my first ever piano solo in church

BELOW: Playing with Jeff Stice at National Quartet Convention

The little church we attended on Christmas Eve in 2012 and sang Christmas carols together

Phil, Olivia and I enjoying a day off in San Francisco - 2017

2014 – Phil & I, along with Cliff & Ann Barrows, at The Cove, Asheville, NC

ABOVE: 2016 – The Collingsworth Family with Dr. David Jeremiah at Shadow Mountain Community Church, El Cajon, CA

RIGHT: 2017 – CFAM goes to Carnegie Hall

BELOW: 2017 – Performing at Carnegie Hall in NYC with Shadow Mountain Choir & Orchestra

ABOVE: 2009 – Special
Evening with Larnelle Harris
& CFAM at Taft Theater,
Cincinnati, Ohio

RIGHT: 2016 – Mixed
Group of the Year and
Musician of the Year
– National Quartet
Convention

2015 – Kim Collingsworth's
MAJESTIC piano project
honored with a Silver Telly
Award

*2015 - With Clarke Beasley,
Executive Director of
the National Quartet
Convention and presenter
of the SILVER TELLY
AWARD*

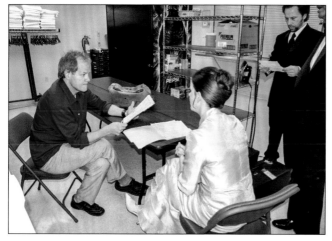

*Last minute
preparation with
Dan Posthuma,
co-producer
of the Piano
Extravaganzas in
Shipshewana, IN*

*Necessary
preparation for
bright lights and
video production*

ABOVE: 2019 – Adding some grandchildren in the mix at National Quartet Convention

LEFT: 2019 - A much needed family vacation

RIGHT: Date night – Cincinnati Reds game – Phil's a big fan!

ABOVE: Black Pearl in tow on the Christmas Tour - 2017

RIGHT: Headed into the Ronald Reagan International Center in Washington DC to sing for the National Day of Prayer kick-off banquet

BELOW: 2019 - National Day of Prayer banquet

TOP: 2019 – The Collingsworth
Family with Dr. James and Shirley
Dobson at the National Day of
Prayer banquet

ABOVE: With my wonderful
parents, James and Carolyn Keaton
- celebrating their 50th wedding
anniversary

RIGHT: Our sweet granddaughter,
Emma Olivia, singing on stage with
Nana

ABOVE: *Playing at National Quartet Convention in Louisville, Kentucky*

RIGHT: *2019 – Last performance of our 20th year of ministry – The White House, Washington DC*

BELOW: *2019 – Inside the White House*

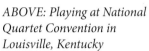

ABOVE: 2019 – Tour of the US Capitol after White House performance

LEFT: 2019 – In the US Capitol building with our friends and tour guides, Congressman Bob & Liz McEwen

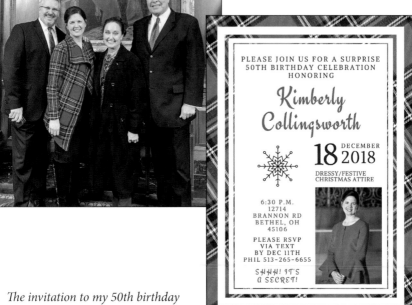

PLEASE JOIN US FOR A SURPRISE
50TH BIRTHDAY CELEBRATION
HONORING

Kimberly
Collingsworth

18 DECEMBER
2018

DRESSY/FESTIVE
CHRISTMAS ATTIRE

6:30 P.M.
12714
BRANNON RD
BETHEL, OH
45106

PLEASE RSVP
VIA TEXT
BY DEC 11TH
PHIL 513-265-6655

SHHH! IT'S
A SECRET!

The invitation to my 50th birthday party - The biggest surprise of my life!

ABOVE: The beautiful grand piano ice sculpture at my surprise 50th birthday party

LEFT: The beautiful cake at my surprise 50th birthday party

A day of arranging with David Clydesdale in Nashville

2019 - Accepting the award for ALBUM OF THE YEAR (Mercy & Love) with our producer, Wayne Haun

ABOVE: The CFAM singing AT CALVARY with The Brooklyn Tabernacle Choir at INSPIRATION ENCOUNTER 2019

LEFT: 2019 – Singing at The Brooklyn Tabernacle, with our dear friends, Pastor Jim and Carol Cymbala

ABOVE: 2020 – performing at NQC Fall Festival / Collingsworth Family Showcase

ABOVE: 2020 – Accepting MUSICIAN OF THE YEAR award – National Quartet Convention

LEFT: 2020 – Preparing for filming with Congressman Bob McEwen in THE HAVEN, our new video suite

ABOVE: 2020 – Singing at
First Baptist Atlanta, Dr.
Charles Stanley's church

RIGHT: 2019 – Christmas
at THE COVE, Asheville,
NC

BELOW: 2020 - The
entire CFAM, back home
in Mt Orab, OH at The
Collingsworth Family
HomePlace

Three weeks later we received an email from a gentleman who had been in the audience that evening. He introduced himself as a physician who had had several guests with him that night, one of whom was a retired NBA player. His first question, somewhat rhetorical, was, "My friend (the NBA player) wants to know, 'Kim, where in the world do you get your joy!?'"

His main purpose for writing, however, was to inquire as to our greatest need. Phil and I both knew of course what that need was, but my immediate response was, "Phil, don't tell him. God promised to provide our *needs*, not our *greeds*. We don't even know if a bus is God's will for the CFAM. Please tell this man that our greatest need is prayer."

Phil thanked the man for his letter and shared our need for prayer. We received a follow up letter a few days later in which he pressed further: "I *know* that you need prayer," he said, "but I'm speaking of a material need. What is it that you need?" Phil read the letter aloud to me, and I trembled inside at these words. "Phil, I wouldn't tell him!" I said and walked out of the office.

Why is it that we pray, and then when God begins to answer we become skittish and unbelieving? I don't know how I thought God would answer our prayer for a bus, but I didn't expect *this*.

Phil carefully crafted his response to read, "Thank you so much for your letter. In answer to your inquiry, the Collingsworth family needs prayer, specifically about transportation. This is a need that you can help us pray about."

Within twenty-four hours we received yet another letter from this gentleman, where he shared with us how God had been working in his life. Just before attending our concert, he had finished a forty-day time of prayer and fasting. He shared how God had asked him during this time if he would be willing to be a "servant" and a "giver". On the night of the concert, he felt God speak to him specifically, *"This family needs help with transportation. Would you be willing to help?"*

Afterward, he discussed this for several weeks with his family. He thought perhaps he was having an impression, and decided to ask us about our needs. He'd put out a fleece of sorts, asking the Lord to have Phil respond with the word "*transportation*" if this was something more than a mere impression.

I'm glad Phil didn't listen to my faithless advice. This doctor gifted us a brand new motorhome with instructions to "do with it whatever you wish." We sold it, and the money from the sale put us into our very first bus, "Big Red!"

Prayer has kept us steady when assaulted by the enemy.

When I was in my twenties, I received a book at a Christmas gift exchange. I put it on my bookshelf, and it was a decade before I redis-covered *The Necessity of Prayer,* by E.M. Bounds. This book, and others he has written on the subject of prayer, have profoundly impacted me.

In this particular book, he states:

> Reading God's Word regularly and praying habitually in the secret place of the Most High, puts one where he is absolutely safe from the attacks of the enemy of souls and guarantees him salvation and final victory through the overcoming power of the Lamb.

I found this truth written in my journal during a difficult time. It was puzzling to me, how when God was doing something amazing and new in our ministry, we'd be assaulted in every conceivable way. I wondered at times if my family believed the stories I'd share of the incredible, cra-zy situations we found ourselves in. Surely our luck couldn't have been that pitiful. I understand now, that when God is working, Satan is never far behind, unleashing his arsenal in attempts to discourage and turn us aside. And boy is he ever creative!

In 2007, I sat down at the piano one day and began to sing a lyric that had recently come to me. As I sang the simple chorus, the verses came quickly. Sometime later we made plans to record it. It was a simple lyric that went like this:

The blood of Jesus,
The blood of Jesus,
The blood of Jesus
Can cleanse your deepest sin.

You may think you've gone too far;
You may think there is no power
That can wash away your deepest sin.
There is hope for you my friend;
Jesus died and rose again
So that you could know the joy of sins forgiv'n.

The blood of Jesus,
The blood of Jesus,
The blood of Jesus
Can cleanse your deepest sin.

You may have some hidden sin
You try to cover deep within,
And everybody thinks your life is in control.
You can run but you can't hide;
God sees everything inside,
But forgiveness waits at the foot of Calvary's cross[6]

On the days leading up to our studio date, I was convinced this song was too simple. It *wasn't* a good lyric—it wasn't going on this album.

I walked into the studio that morning and told Wayne Haun, our producer that everything would be recorded as planned except for this song. "*Kim*, are you *serious*?" He asked incredulously. "You *have* to record this song!" I acquiesced, and with some reservation we recorded, "The Blood of Jesus."

We began to sing this song in concert, and the response was incredible. God anointed the simple Gospel, and I was amazed and humbled.

6 The Collingsworth Family, *The Blood of Jesus*, track # 1, We Still Believe, Crossroads Records, 2007, CD

But I will never forget the fury unleashed on our family during the ten-day period wherein "The Blood of Jesus" was released.

It began with the discovery of five hundred bats living in our attic. When the exterminators came and began their treatment the bats, having been driven from their attic home, began dive-bombing our windows. It was terrifying! The $5,000 invoice they left behind was even more disturbing!

The very next day, Phil had four new tires put on his truck. He was traveling home on a rural road at about 55 mph, when the front wheel flew off and headed for the picture window of a brick ranch home where two elderly people were sitting. Thankfully, the wheel glanced off a tree and hit their truck and car instead, causing several thousand dollars damage. Phil careened down the road on the hub, with sparks flying five feet high next to his window, narrowly escaping a serious accident.

He rented a truck and while driving the next day, a distracted driver crashed into our rental.

We were to leave the following evening, so while Phil dealt with the rental truck situation, I packed the bus. In those days, we had no parking space for the bus at our home, and we parked it at a little Baptist church two miles away. I made multiple trips that day carrying towels, sheets, and stage clothes. I carefully packed the kids individual book bags with needed homework assignments to be completed as we traveled. I hauled lunch meat, cheese, bread, milk, cereal, and toiletries, and by the time we were prepared to head out it was 1:00 a.m.

I headed to the back of the bus exhausted but feeling satisfied. We were on the bus, the kids were in their bunks, and my work for today was finished. I anticipated my bus bed, with the familiar hum of the engine beneath me, a sound which never failed to lull me into a deep, dreamless sleep; a place where bats and flying tires couldn't interrupt.

My sense of well-being was short-lived when Phil informed me that he couldn't find his laptop. He was frantic because he had also placed the master tracks to all of our music in the laptop bag. He feared that when

he had returned the rental truck earlier in the day, he had carelessly left
the bag lying on the ground. It would be a forty-five-minute drive in the
opposite direction to return to the truck rental office. I retired to the
bedroom, too weary and stressed to handle another emergency. When
we arrived back at the rental location, sure enough, the laptop bag was
not only on the ground, but had been run over when he had pulled out
earlier! The computer was smashed in pieces, but miraculously, the master tracks weren't damaged at all. *Thank you, Lord!*

A few days later, while rolling down the road to our next concert
venue, I smelled an acrid burning smell. After stopping to check things
out, Phil and Lowell (our bus driver) assured me that all was well. I
looked at both of them dubiously, still sure that something was amiss. It
wasn't until later that afternoon, and after discovering we had no water,
that Phil opened the bay to find there had been a large fire. Thankfully,
our water tank, which had contained three hundred gallons of water, had
put the fire out after a hole burned through it. We were grateful that we
had been spared a more tragic outcome.

Despite the dreadful inconveniences of the week, God helped us tremendously that evening, and the concert was blessed with His anointing
and sweet presence.

That night after greeting people, we headed down the road for an
overnight drive to our next venue. I had just drifted off to sleep when a
loud bang startled me awake. I stumbled out of bed and lurched down
the aisle, through the kids' bunk room, and to the front just as our driver
called out frantically, "We're going to get hit!" We had blown a tire in a
construction zone on the Pennsylvania Turnpike with no place to get off
the road. Large semis swerved around us, as we had slowed dramatically.
Relief washed over me when I saw a Flying J truck stop up ahead, but my
relief was short-lived. We pulled in and around the building noticing the
"Grand Opening" signs and balloons. What we didn't realize was that
our blown tire rim was "christening" the brand-new parking lot, grind-
ing a deep rut in the fresh asphalt. It was a humiliating moment when

the manager ran out yelling like a madman, "You're gonna pay for every dime of this damage!" We apologized profusely and gave our insurance information. But they never did bother to file a claim.

I'll never forget, though, that as we sang in Salisbury, Maryland, that afternoon, I spoke to the crowd for three or four minutes and shared the simple Gospel. I felt compelled to assure someone in the audience that Jesus' blood was still powerful to forgive, cleanse, and deliver from the bondage of sin. We sang our newly released song, "The Blood of Jesus," and God's Spirit filled the house.

I have never forgotten a young woman who approached me after the concert. God had so powerfully moved upon her by His Spirit. As she wept on my shoulder, she shared that she was not supposed to have been there that day. Someone had urged her to come and she had decided, on a whim, to drive the 150 miles. The music, the message, and mostly the presence of God had profoundly impacted and encouraged her that day. I believe she was one of many.

I was reminded that afternoon of the "why." Life on the road is far from glamorous, and those past ten days had been fraught with difficulty, stress, and financial setbacks. There had been days when I opened my eyes and said, "Phil, I'm afraid to get out of bed." We felt we had been in an all out war with the Enemy. Lest you think I'm being dramatic, I'll remind you that God's Word assures us that, "...our struggle is not against flesh and blood, but against the rulers, against the authorities, against the powers of this dark world and against the spiritual forces of evil in the heavenly realms" (Ephesians 6:12). We were reminded, once again, of the necessity of putting on the armor of God *every day; of remaining steadfastly* in the Word, of bathing our lives and ministry in prayer.

As Phil and I reflected over our struggles, we began to trace the hand of God. We saw that in each instance, Satan had hurled his arrows, but God had carried us through, worked things out, and made a way. Satan did not get the final word. Mr. Bounds was right—we *were, "absolutely safe from the attacks of the enemy of souls,"* and we had been given, *"salvation and final victory through the overcoming power of the Lamb."*

Have Phil and I ever skipped our prayer meetings? Absolutely. There have been seasons when life became so busy—on the road, in the studio, or just life—and we'd realize that we had missed one or two or even three Tuesday prayer meetings. But our desperate need for communion with God, *together*, has pulled us back to the place of prayer time and again. This need has caused us to rearrange our schedules to make time for prayer. It has sometimes propelled me to the front of the bus for midnight prayer meetings while Phil drives, or driven us both to the back room for time to seek our Father's face together.

This is not a legalistic practice; it is not a magic wand, but it *is* the *lifeline* of our lives and ministry.

Prayer is the "secret" of success

I am privileged to meet many young aspiring artists—people who are very gifted and have much to offer. One of the questions I hear most often is this: "How can *we* do what *you* do?" It is wonderful to talk with these young people and share any practical wisdom I may have. I love their earnest desire, and I want to be faithful and to be a good example. I am all about working hard, pursuing excellence, honing gifts and skills God has given, and walking through open doors. What I want others to understand *most*, however, is the importance of prayer—of seeking God's face, of understanding that we are utterly dependent upon him for success. I have often ended conversations with young artists by challenging them to do three things.

First, pray.
Second, pray.
Third, pray.

The longer I live, the more I know prayer is the key. The starry eyed artists, enamored by stage lights, traveling the country on a big bus, or seeing their names on a marque, will surely be disillusioned. It's in the secret place that one's calling is affirmed, God's grace received, and one's faith strengthened to believe that He who has called us also assumes responsibility for us.

I know well there will come a day when I'll be *old*. I won't be beating the road from the back of a bus forever. Another will take my place on the stage. Sometimes I've wondered, *"How will I feel then?"*

When that day comes, I want to be enjoying the fruit of a lifelong pursuit of a deep and intimate relationship with my Heavenly Father. I want to be spoiled by His presence, His voice, and His gentle, "Well done." I want to spend my remaining days telling my grandchildren that God is real and He is good. I want to regale the generations who follow me with *God* stories that will make *Him* look just as good and strong and kind as I have found Him to be. I want my feet to be planted firmly in my identity as the daughter of the King. Can there be anything greater?

7

HOW DID WE DO THAT?

Train up a child in the way he should go,
but be sure you go that way yourself.
—Charles Spurgeon

June 26, 2004

Right now, we are in Adrian, Michigan. It's Saturday night, and Phil is at the church setting up. I have the kids in a motel, getting ready for Sunday. I've got the cooler packed for lunch tomorrow, and most of the clothes ironed. I bought a candle and a game of checkers at Family Dollar tonight, and the kids are having a checkers tournament. These rooms aren't the greatest, so we're burning candles to help. You've gotta cheer things up and make it homey on the road.

Reading this journal entry took me back with a wave of nostalgia to those early days. We didn't have a bus, so I'd prepare our outfits for the weekend and hang them in the back of the trailer bundled together by concert. Phil would just have to grab one bundle each night, which included everyone's clothing for that concert. The kids each had their own spot in the van, and I took them shopping and let each child pick out their own fabric from which I had "road" blankets made. They were made of soft flannel, and I loved knowing the kids were cozy on those long trips home at the end of busy weekends. Part of our packing routine was putting the kid's blankets, pillows, and book bags in their seats. We'd travel late before stopping to sleep, and since we didn't have cell phones or reservations back in the day, we'd pull under the porticos of random motels, and I'd wait while Phil checked us in, after which we'd both half-carry our sleepy kids in and put them to bed.

Often, Phil would have to get up early and run to the church to set up the sound equipment. Before going, he'd bring up a complimentary breakfast tray; I'd feed and supervise while the kids got dressed for church. Phil would come racing in with minutes to spare, grab a shower, and get dressed. Phillip was a bit young for setup in the beginning, and we had no help. It was just us! Or maybe I should say, "just Phil." He worked so hard, yet had energy to spare. He often jokes that Phillip's 6' 4" frame is a direct answer to his prayers. He needed a helper!

After each concert, we took time to greet the people before "tearing" things down and packing up. As we headed down the road I'd get in the back with the children and open the cooler I'd packed with sandwiches, fruit, gogurts, chips, and on Sunday's, a small amount of candy. I'd pass a plate of food up to Phil and each of the kids, and we'd eat as we sailed down the highway toward our next venue. I don't know *how* we did it! Actually, I do. We relied on the grace and strength of God. We were in the center of His will and we were happy.

We arrived at our hotel late one evening. The kids and I would typically wait in the car until Phil had us all checked in. On this night, two-and-a-half-year-old Phillip wanted to go with daddy, so we unbuckled his car seat and he leaped down and excitedly scampered inside with Phil. He loved being with "Daddy," and stood by Phil's pant leg at the front desk while he secured our room for the night. Phil stood chatting with the hotel clerk, until she stopped him mid-sentence and said with alarm, "What's that noise?" And then, "Sir, where's your little boy!?" Phillip had vanished! Phil panicked when he noticed the pool in the adjacent room. He headed there at a dead run, and found Phillip at the bottom of the hot tub, all tangled up in the black tarp that had covered it. Phil pulled him from the water, and a stunned child and terrified dad made their way back out to the car. Phillip coughed a little, and with wide eyes stated, "I baptized myself!" We laughed, but both Phil and I trembled for days following this near tragedy. We thanked God for His protection.

The logistics even back then were daunting. And when working on a recording project, plus keeping our regular concert schedules, and parenting four growing kids, there were times I felt pushed to near exhaustion. During the recording of our first family album, I wrote the following entry in my journal:

> This has been quite a week! I spent thirty-one hours in the studio and finished our vocals. Thank God! We sang three times this weekend, Friday, Saturday, and Sunday. We were so tired by Sunday night we hardly knew what to do. God helped us so much in spite of our weakness.
>
> I was hoarse so much of the week, but every time I got into the studio God touched my voice, and I was able to sing freely. Thank you, Lord.

It seemed that every time we were set to record, one of us would lose our voice. This used to send me into a panic, but not any more. I have watched God heal our voices dozens of times, and have learned to send a prayer heavenward, sip some herbal tea, drink some straight grapefruit juice, and wait on the Lord.

Traversing the country with our children didn't exclude them from the normal childhood illnesses and mishaps, which are much easier to handle at home. One night we sang in New Castle, Pennsylvania. The crowd was large, but my mother's heart was hurting because 10-year old Courtney was suffering a terrible earache. I can still see her face wet with tears as she tried to stifle her sobs while I made her as comfortable as possible on an empty pew in the back of the sanctuary, praying she would fall asleep. I felt so *guilty* as I made my way to the front of the building. And I wasn't immune to the voices in my head, accusing me with thoughts such as, *What are we doing out here! This isn't normal! Our child is sick, and we're hundreds of miles from home and our pediatrician.* By the time the concert was over, clinics were closed, and we didn't want to visit an emergency room due to having no health insurance at the time. We fervently prayed and asked the Lord to help us and to *please touch Courtney.* We stopped at a Walmart to purchase ear drops and pain medication to get us through the night. Phil stayed in the car with the kids, and when I came out fifteen minutes later to rejoin them, Courtney's pain had *vanished.* She stated, "Mommy, Jesus touched me." And He had. We went to sleep that night feeling loved and cared for by God, and grateful that our children had also witnessed this answer to our prayer.

I have always loved what we do—sharing the Gospel through music. But especially in the early years, there was a bit of a dichotomy that I wrestled with. There was the sheer joy of standing on stage with my family, of experiencing God's presence as we sang together, of witnessing the faces of people being encouraged and challenged by the message and music, and of hearing their heartwarming and sometimes heartrending stories afterwards, contrasted with the mind numbing effort involved in making it all happen. I'm sure other artists would agree that the "standing-on-stage-singing" part of the ministry is about ten percent of what we actually do. The other ninety percent is much less glamorous, and downright grueling at times.

God was always working with me, helping me to learn how to rest in Him. I wrote in my journal something Elizabeth George so aptly wrote:

> If you desire to have a good life, focus on having one good day, one quality day today. Every day is a little life, and our whole life is but a single day repeated.

God helped me to understand that I could be successful in this crazy, hectic, sometimes upside-down world of traveling; that if my kids were up half the night, the world wouldn't end; that if they sometimes had breakfast at noon and dinner at midnight, it was okay. I could thrive and make *these* days *good* days, even while our life wasn't "normal" compared to the lifestyles of other families.

God revealed to me a beautiful truth about my questioning the "normalcy" of our lives. One day I felt Him say to me, "*Normal?* Normal is whatever I call you to do—that is *your* normal; embrace it, make the best of it. Do not compare yourselves to others."

How wonderful and freeing it was for me. And it can be for you, too! I have a feeling that, though my circumstances may be different from yours, we all struggle with similar concerns. The paths of other people often look easier, more glamorous, less stressful, but it's not true. Every path leads through valleys. If you are in the center of God's will, stay put. He has wonderful things to show you right where you are.

This was a season of surrender in my life—a time when God helped me to stop resisting the difficulties, and embrace this life and calling with all my heart. One afternoon I penned the following words. They came fast and furious and from a deep longing in my heart. Although we've not yet recorded this song, it is my testimony:

> It's easy to commit to things that I can touch and see,
> But a different thing to be surrendered
> To whatever he wants from me.
> When I don't understand my future,
> And I can't figure out his plan,
> I choose to let go,
> Let him have control,
> And place my life in His hands.
>
> I surrender, with no demands;
> I surrender, take my life, my dreams, and my plans.
> I don't know where it will lead me;
> I rest in your hands, and that's alright with me;
> I surrender, with no demands.

I've heard the word, 'surrender'
Far back as my mind can think.
But I didn't comprehend the meaning
Or what it meant for me personally.
Then one day I came to a crossroads;
A war raged inside of me.
I heard a voice gently call,
"Give me your all,"
And I fell on my knees and said,

I surrender, with no demands;
I surrender, take my life, my dreams, and my plans.
I don't know where it will lead me;
I rest in your hands, and that's alright with me;
I surrender, with no demands.[7]

I recorded the following truth from E. M. Bounds in my journal:

"The consecrated soul is the happiest soul."

Please Excuse Us While our Children Grow Up!

There were times I wished for a magic wand of "good behavior" to wave over my children so they would always act as pretty as they looked on stage. When young, they engaged in the normal backstage bickering from time to time. I remember being asked, "Do your kids ever fight?" I had to smile and admit the truth. Although, we did have a standing rule that no one dared walk on that stage with any disturbance between them and another member of the family.

This has been a beautiful thing to see—Phillip telling Olivia "sorry" and that... *she wasn't really adopted from a family of red-headed leprechauns*; or others working out a previous disagreement before we prayed together just prior to singing. And Phil and I have had plenty of

---

7 Kim Collingsworth, *No Demands*, 2006

opportunities to demonstrate this over the years. Although the children are grown and get along well, we *all* still clear any cluttered air before singing. We believe God both understands our *humanity and* rewards our *humility*.

Traveling with children has its share of embarrassing moments. We were in a certain city and doing the music for a women's conference. After having been cooped up in the van for hours, Phillip, perhaps nine at the time, couldn't wait to try out his new football. We arrived at the venue where several hundred ladies had gathered for some... *rest and repose*. Well, Phillip opened the van door and jumped out, ready to try his arm at a long pass. In his enthusiasm, he failed to see the two ladies walking across the lawn. Now, I don't know their stories, but I can just imagine they had left their own unruly "savages" at home, and were anticipating a reprieve from the jungle. I hardly think either of those dear ladies planned on being a "wide receiver" that weekend! And I don't know what Phillip's rationale was for his next action, or if nine-year-old boys even possess such a thing, but... he threw one deep! And the poor lady ended up with a sore face and broken glasses. I think my face was as red as hers!

As the children grew, and life got busier with the ministry, I was constantly endeavoring to maintain balance in my life. I am quite task oriented, and I sometimes struggled to maintain symmetry between keeping our lives highly organized, being a loving wife and gentle mom, and pushing for excellence in our music—which included weekly music lessons and substantial amounts of rehearsal time. I wrote in my journal:

> God is showing me that it is the "little foxes" that spoil the vine. I want to make sure that I am not eating the bread of idleness. I must stay focused on my husband, my children, and my prayer and devotional time. This is what gives me the strength to wear so many hats.

One of my favorite verses in the Bible is Colossians 3:15, "And let the peace of God rule in your hearts, since as members of one body you were called to peace. And be thankful." During some of those grueling days, as I became so focused on the tasks that had to be done, God began to show me that creating and maintaining an atmosphere of peace in our home (or on the bus) was equally as important as getting things done. I realized that my "law and order" attitude sometimes took the peace and fun right out of our lives. My intensity sometimes caused the peace in our home to dissipate, and in order for us to work together, live on a bus together, and still have fun together, there had to be peace.

E. M. Bounds wrote the following that I recorded in my journal:

> "The most effective teaching or preaching [or singing] is not that which is heard from the pulpit, but that which is proclaimed quietly, humbly, and consistently, which exhibits its excellency in the home or the community."

This was profound to me, and impressed upon me the importance of living a godly, prayerful life when the lights were off, when there was no stage, no applauding audience, no acclaim. Living righteously and peacefully as I walked through the mundanity of life as a wife, mother, sister, daughter, or friend—this is what mattered most. It is still what matters most!

I ran across the following poem on one of those tough days and put it to memory! I think I even quoted it a time or two from the stage. It impacted me so much because, though it is simple, the truth hit me right where I was living.

Myself

I have to live with myself and so
I want to be fit for myself to know.
I want to be able as days go by,
Always to look myself straight in the eye;
I don't want to stand with the setting sun
And hate myself for the things I have done.

I don't want to keep on a closet shelf
A lot of secrets about myself.
I cannot fool myself as I come and go
Into thinking no one else will ever know
The kind of person I really am;
I don't want to dress up myself in sham.
I want to go out with my head erect,
I want to deserve all men's respect;
Here in the struggle for fame and wealth
I want to be able to like myself.
I don't want to look at myself and know
I am bluster and bluff and empty show.
I never can hide myself from me;
I see what others may never see;
I know what others may never know,
I cannot fool myself and so,
Whatever happens I want to be
Self-respecting and conscience free.
(Edgar A. Guest)

A few years into our full-time concert schedule, the kids were growing up, and we were singing 100 dates per year. Brooklyn was now a teenager, and we sensed she was beginning to feel the sting of "missing out." Our church affiliation had two wonderful events geared towards young people each year, and as we prayed for our children we sensed they needed to be involved. During our prayer meeting and talk time, Phil and I made a decision that we would arrange our schedule to accommodate these dates, and we would experience these occasions *with* our kids.

In the following years, each July would find us pulling the bus into the campground in Roxbury, Pennsylvania, so our teens could spend a week at their favorite youth camp. I'd fill our cupboards and fridge with snacks and drinks so the kids could bring their friends on the bus to hang out. They played softball and volleyball, and heard wonderful music and preaching during the morning and evening services. They made memories that will last a lifetime.

Each October, we were home for Youth Challenge, a fun-filled, two-day youth event that was founded by our daughter-in-law's father, Rev. Tim Dotson. Our children looked forward to these events, and it gave them a sense of belonging that was important. And although this was not intended, both Brooklyn and Courtney met their future husbands there. We also made sure we were able to attend our large church convention in Dayton, Ohio, each April as well. The kids loved reconnecting with friends, and we were grateful for the truth-filled messages they heard in these services.

Our four were (still are) blessed with some great friends. I loved hosting groups of them for birthday parties and Friday night get-togethers when we were home. I even joined in for a few harrowing games of after-dark, "Capture the Flag." And Brooklyn still declares she doesn't know if she was proud or embarrassed when, on her twelfth birthday, I joined her and her friends for a game of softball, and hit a home run.

While on tour in Florida each February, we tried to schedule a few days for fun. Once, we were given tickets to Disney World, and this was especially exciting for the children. We had a favorite family-friendly resort where we'd spend a few days, and Phil and I joined the kids on go-carts and Ferris wheels. We played putt-putt, and enjoyed hamburgers and ice cream on warm evenings. These were wonderful days of stepping away from the intensity of singing and all the logistics involved. I'd schedule these days to be "break days" from school, which always made the kids happy.

Years ago, as a young wife, I asked God to bless me with children. I went a step further, and asked if I could please spend more time with *mine* than I had with *my* parents as a teenager. It was a simple request, and spoken without even a hint of resentment; only a sadness of what I had missed. God graciously granted this, and the days of doing life, ministry, and family all together, still remain one of the greatest blessings in my life. Today, I cherish the fact that, though the children are grown, they are still heavily invested in the ministry. I know that things could, and probably will change someday. And when the time comes, it will be okay. But for today...I'll relish the moments.

Life in the CFAM Academy

In July of 2016, while looking over our schedule for the month, I noted there was one item I wouldn't be adding to the calendar. This year I wouldn't be ordering *school curriculum*! How could it *be*? After nineteen grueling years of homeschooling, I was finished. With Olivia's graduation from high school in May, I had wrapped up that chapter of life.

My role as a homeschooling mom was something that was behind the scenes; not something people think of when they see our family on stage. Nevertheless, it has always been one of my greatest priorities, and consumed much of my time and energy. I felt a wave of profound sadness...for about fifteen minutes! And then I went shopping!

I'd never intended to homeschool my children, and I had no idea in the early days of our ministry that homeschool would be a necessity for our family. I'm forever grateful for a wonderful lady, whom God sent into my life, who opened up the possibilities of this brave new world of home education.

When our three older children were small, I taught a few piano students from home. Diana Metz, the mother of one of my students, had been a public-school teacher, but became a homeschooling mom, educating all four of her daughters. In my eyes she was the essence of what a home educator should be—fun, vivacious, creative, and smart. She was the homeschool mom who churned butter with her children, then studied the chemistry of how the butter-churning process worked. She seized every moment as a teachable moment.

One day while we talked together, I mentioned that we had enrolled Brooklyn in a local private kindergarten but that I was having second thoughts. The $159 per month was a stretch for our budget in those early days of ministry, and I'm not sure what I expected kindergarten to be, but I remember thinking they did a lot of coloring! Diana looked at me that day and said, "Kim, *you* could teach your daughter how to read." I almost laughed out loud! *Me!? Homeschool!?*

I recalled my own educational experience. I wanted more for my children. Every generation does.

I had attended private schools—good schools—but music was my priority. School days were often punctuated by interruptions. I'd be called out of class, sometimes every day, for rehearsals or performances. To me, math, science, English, and history were necessary, but always *secondary*. Much of the time, I took my assignments on the road as I traveled with various singing groups. I found the following written in my journal from the sixth grade. I was eleven years old and in large childish handwriting I wrote:

> March 1981,
>   David Miller came today and recorded Ben and me playing for the kids for the state convention. Then I had to stay over there (at the church) until one p.m. I went back to the school and did my schoolwork.
>   Bye

Ben Colburn was a church organist, old enough to have been my father. The "kids" I referred to were actually high school seniors. *(I must have been an old soul)*. That was the school year in which I played for chapel each week; also the year I suffered the humiliation of having a piano bench break while playing the piano in front of the entire student body. I had fallen to the floor with a crash!

It may seem hard to believe, but as a young child I was quite mischievous in school—so much so that my teacher once showed up at our home...*unannounced*...to speak with my parents about my bad behavior.

I meant no harm when in the fifth grade I gathered a team of "helpers" and we covered all the plants in our classroom with shaving cream. I realize now that destroying our teacher's favorite "students"—as she called her plants—was reprehensible. At some point in my teenage years, I wrote this dear lady a letter of apology. She forgave me!

In the following journal entry, I talk a little about my 'trouble" at school:

> Today, I had a terrible day at school because I got six demerits! We practiced our ensemble today and had tacos for supper.

I'm not sure what the six demerits were for *that* time! I guess whatever it was, it didn't hinder me from my music.

In high school I had great teachers and a principal who worked closely with me to ensure that I completed all the necessary classes. School was stressful, however; something I had to fit into the busy schedule of life on the road. I remember sitting in a science class while our teacher held up glass vials with various pale liquids in them. I was bored, and my mind wandered. In the course of the lecture, the teacher tapped the side of one of those vials, and my first thought was, *that's a D flat.* I struggled with math, and X+Y equaled chaos to me!

I approached our principal at the beginning of my junior year, and asked if I could double up on my classes. "I want to finish up two years in one," I said. He understood my situation, said he was open to the idea, and helped me make a plan. I told my brother Jeff, who was just a year ahead of me. "You can't do it!" he scoffed. That response, coupled with the prospect of graduating and getting to marry Phil, was just the challenge I needed. I worked night and day on the road, and late into the night when I was home. And I did it!

When just a few months later, I donned my cap and gown and marched down the aisle to "Pomp and Circumstance," Jeff was just in front of me. I must admit I had a very strong urge to give him a swift kick in the seat of the pants, and an *"I told you I could do this!"*

Is it any wonder I didn't view myself as "homeschool mom" material? Diana encouraged me, introduced me to a music-based curriculum, and walked the journey with me for years.

I have been asked dozens of times, "How do you homeschool and keep up while traveling?" It was grace. Not only did God send me an encourager and counselor in Diana, but each time I felt over my head— hundreds of times—I asked Him to help me. I felt my own inadequacy. I didn't want my children to be dumb! It sounds funny, but it's true. I wondered how in the world I could do this, and yet, it *was* necessary. I remember God guiding me to Matthew 6:33, which has become my all-time life verse. It says "Seek ye first the kingdom of God and His righteousness, and all these things shall be added to you" (KJV). I have placed many things in that "all" category, and the education of my children was one of them. I was seeking God first, so I asked Him to help me be diligent, disciplined, and methodical in my approach to this seemingly impossible undertaking. And then I got to work.

One of the most important elements of mothering is prioritizing. I am not unlike other moms. We wear so many different hats as moms, and we want to wear each of them well. I've discovered, however, that in order to maximize our impact, we must prayerfully decide which things are *most* important, and then give those things their due diligence. I felt deeply that I mustn't be cavalier regarding my children's schooling; that this is something I *must* do well.

I mentioned earlier that Phil and I came to the agreement that I would "own" Monday through Thursday. Knowing these days would be spent at home—where I could educate the children in an organized way—was crucial. If any concert requests came in for those days, Phil always deferred to me. I had the final say. And there were times when we worked it out and took the dates, but there were more times that we declined.

On the rare occasions when we traveled during the week, I took the kids schoolwork along, and tried my best to make sure they completed their weekly assignments. On one such occasion we sang for a conference at Wesley Biblical Seminary in Jackson, Mississippi. We sang several times a day after which the speakers would lecture. I recorded that two of the speakers were Dr. H. B. London and Dr. Thane Ury. I found the following journal entry from that particular week.

> This has been a very busy two and a half days; I've been running like crazy just trying to get ready for the next session. Tuesday night we put the kids in a small coat room in the foyer of WBS and they worked on schoolwork. I felt sorry for them.

Is it any wonder I loved my weekdays at home? My poor children!

As the CFAM ministry began to grow, there were other opportunities that could have pulled me away. I began to receive invitations to speak at different churches and women's conferences. This was flattering but, honestly, I wondered why people thought I had something to say. I was just powering through my days with my head down. I was, myself, gleaning all I could from good books (Elizabeth George, was my favorite author in those days), my homeschool mentor, and others. Nevertheless, the invitations came, and I remember clearly hearing God's voice as he instructed me, "Kim, not now; this is not your season." It was as if God said, "I didn't call you to speak, I gave you four children—now get to it!" I instructed our office manager to graciously decline any such offers. Although these invites were good things—wonderful opportunities—I knew that to accept them would mean lots of preparation, which equals time—time that I needed to invest in my children and the music ministry God had called us to. I felt such peace when I made that decision. I would write in my journal:

> God, please help me to have a strong constitution when it comes to mothering my children and saying "no" to all the demands around me. Help me to remain entirely focused on this season of my life.

I learned to be organized. This is something Diana helped me with. She showed me the scope and sequence of what my children needed to know in each grade. She taught me the importance of mapping out our school year. This would take days to do but it gave me such a feeling of satisfaction to see the one hundred eighty days carefully planned on the calendar, and the realization that getting this done was possible.

I also learned that flexibility in the midst of structure was important as well. My school calendar was revamped throughout the year, and days moved around as needed. If we got in at 4 a.m. on Monday morning, I didn't require the kids to be in the school room at 8 a.m. That's border-line child abuse! We would just start in the afternoon and work until we were finished. I was a big fan of the modern day beatitude, "Blessed are the flexible, for they shall not break."

I'm sure there are others who would do things differently, but I thrived on structure. This is why my kids had to be up and fully dressed for school. There was something about sitting around in our "PJ's" that made me feel unproductive. Perhaps I was afraid the kids' math papers would resemble their hair. We had a schoolroom with a table where the children worked. I'd sit at my desk and write newsletters or thank you notes for the ministry, plan menus, and make grocery lists, all the while keeping an eye on the kids. Sometimes, I'd have to work to keep them on task, or send Courtney to the "principal's" (Phil's) office for distracting the others by inserting pencils up her nose, or some such escapade. There were days when I'd loved to have seen a yellow school bus pull up out front to take them away, but this wasn't to be. As the years passed, I leaned into this reality, and learned to enjoy the moments—or most of them. But by most Thursday nights, we were all ready to get on that bus!

I need to pause and give kudos to Phil. He always seemed to know when I needed a healthy diversion. There were times when I'd wake up in the morning and begin the day's routine, but he'd somehow produce money, with instructions that he didn't want to see me until ten o'clock that night. When I'd protest and begin listing all the things we needed to accomplish in school that day, he'd gently shush me, tell me he'd oversee everything, and then send me on my way. Those days were wonderful. I'd come home feeling refreshed and ready to tackle the details of life again. And I'm sure a day away from mom didn't hurt the kids either!

Brooklyn and I suffered through Algebra I and II together. And by the time Olivia finished high school I was—well...let's just say, *thankful!* Phil could have helped us, as he is a whiz at higher math, but he's too smart to teach it. The kids could never understand his methods. He helped with history and Bible. He taught American Government one election year and had Olivia study the electoral college. She made a map of all fifty states, and made projections for how the election would go based upon the electoral votes by states. On election night, they pulled out her projections and compared them with the actual outcome. It was fascinating!

There were days—many of them—when I doubted my ability to continue. I'd pray and ask God for his grace. James 1:5 was my verse in those days. I'd sometimes go into my room and pray this verse to the Lord, prefacing it with "God you promised that, 'If any of you lacks wisdom, let him ask of God who gives to all liberally and without reproach, and it will be given to him" (NKJV). I held God to his Word. I wanted my children to have a good education, and I didn't want to be the one to mess that up. God gave wisdom in many ways. Whether it was through reading the right book or article that addressed my need, or perhaps a word from my mentor or a friend. I've shared this verse with many discouraged and overwhelmed homeschool moms over the years, encouraging them to seek wisdom from the Lord.

A few years ago, I sat and watched our first-born march down the aisle to receive her college diploma, having made the dean's list all but one semester. I was one among thousands there celebrating that day, but this was personal! Tears streamed down my face as I ruminated on the faithfulness of God. I realized Matthew 6:33—that promise given to me so many years before—was playing out before my eyes. Seek his kingdom first, and he will add *all* things. "Kim," I felt him whisper, "You took care of what mattered to me, and today you see I have taken care of what matters to you." Things were coming full circle for me, and it was indeed a moment I won't soon forget.

Perhaps you are reading this and you are a discouraged homeschool mom. Maybe you came home from co-op this week feeling two inches tall after comparing yourself to the other moms who seemingly had it all together. Perhaps even today, you've sat at the kitchen table and cried because you couldn't remember how to do long division, and you wonder if your fourth grader will ever graduate high school.

Trust me, I've been there. So, if I may, let me encourage you by saying that if God has called you to this work, He will see you through. Your job is to do your best, be faithful, be consistent, and be diligent. Get up every day with purpose in your heart to do the work set before you.

And when you don't know what to do, cry out to your Heavenly Father for wisdom and a path forward. He will never let you down.

And let me pass on a bit of practical advice in the words of my own mother. She often advised young moms to learn how to "take five minute vacations—grab a donut and put your feet up." It works wonders every time.

And finally, don't forget to enjoy the journey. I know it sounds cliched, but those little people you have at your table today will be walking out the door tomorrow. Stamp the truth of God upon their hearts, love them unconditionally, show them Jesus every single day, and you will someday reap a beautiful reward.

8

SITTING AT THE END OF THE TABLE

I want a principle within of jealous, godly fear,
a sensibility of sin, a pain to feel it near.
—Charles Wesley

As a little girl, I always looked forward to suppertime. Our family meals around the table promised to be lively times of discussion, laughter, simple but delicious food, and *togetherness*.

As mentioned previously, we had a custom-made table with long benches on either side. There was never any bickering between the nine of us over where we children would sit as we gathered to eat. Dad circumvented that issue by assigning a seat to each of us. My oldest brother, Jimmy, sat on dad's right with my three remaining brothers, Jeff, Troy, and Brian, following according to age. Likewise, my oldest sister, Sandy, sat beside dad on his left with the rest of us girls, Vicky, myself, Becky, and Julia in succession. Being the third oldest daughter, my place was right in the middle. Had I tried to sit next to dad, Sandy would have let me know *in a hurry* that I was in her place! We were equally loved and cared for by our parents, but this was just how it was at suppertime. We each knew our place at the table and learned to be comfortable there.

What was true at our family table is true in life and ministry too. Every Christian's place in the Kingdom is determined by our Heavenly Father, and we must learn to be content in the place He sits us down. And, He will never invite us *up*, unless we prove willing to sit *down*! Jesus taught us this.

One day, Jesus was invited to a dinner party at the home of a prominent Pharisee. While the other invited guests seated themselves, Jesus observed how they scrambled for the most honorable seats at the table. He rebuked this behavior with a story:

> "When someone invites you to a wedding feast, do not take the place of honor, for a person more distinguished than you may have been invited.
>
> If so, the host who invited both of you will come and say to you, 'Give this person your seat.' Then, humiliated, you will have to take the least important place.
>
> But when you are invited, take the lowest place, so that when your host comes he will say to you, 'Friend, move up to a better place.' Then you will be honored in the presence of all your fellow guests.
>
> For all those who exalt themselves will be humbled, and those who humble themselves will be exalted" (Luke 14:8-11).

I can't imagine the burning faces of those at the table who knew Jesus was on to them. These were religious people, yet Jesus saw *right through them.*

Jesus taught that *humility is always the best way.* He minced no words when He taught on the topic, and His teaching ran cross-grain to culture. It still does!

In Matthew 23:12, Jesus told the crowd and His disciples, "Whoever exalts himself will be humbled, and whoever humbles himself will be exalted." Most poignantly, Jesus Himself exemplified humility:

> "Rather, He made himself nothing, taking the very nature of a servant, being made in human likeness. And being found in appearance as a man, He humbled himself by becoming obedient to death—even death on a cross!" (Philippians 2:7-8).

Jesus' way of thinking pierces through the subtlety of our pride and human positioning. It's not *normal* to *choose* the low place, but we must. Quite naturally, I think, we all want to be known and respected, but this God-given desire can so quickly turn to pride—self-promotion, self-aggrandizement, self-interest. Too often, we base our feelings of worth and belonging on which place we're given at the table, so we're tempted to push ourselves forward. In my own life, I've found Jesus is always more interested in humility than in my proximity to some coveted *(sometimes superficial)* seat of honor.

The story of Jesus at the dinner party came to me with fresh meaning early on in the CFAM concert ministry. Stepping out in such an out-of-the-box way (for us) was intimidating. Phil and I were known and loved in our church circles. As we began following God's leading into new places, and meeting many new people, God began afresh to test and refine our motives.

The term "concert ministry" may conjure up images of packed out arenas and adoring fans, but for us, it was often changing into our concert clothes in a church Sunday school room, and peering out the window in hopes that perhaps one more car would drive into a lonely-looking parking lot. It was coming up with the answer to Brooklyn's question one evening as I combed her hair: "Mommy, do you think we will always sing to small crowds?" I'm sure I gave her the "right" answer—that it didn't matter and that we were to do our best, but I will say unashamedly that I sometimes wondered the same thing.

I won't forget being excited to sing in a certain city in Florida. In my mind's eye I can still see the kids and me standing just inside the hotel lobby, dressed to the nines, and waiting for Phil to return from the venue—an old but beautiful theatre where he had gone earlier in the day to set up. The promoter, too, had been exuberant and excited to have The Collingsworth Family for an evening concert. It had promised to be a great night!

We arrived just forty-five minutes before the concert was to begin.

We entered the foyer of the theatre, and noted the tired charm of the place. There was a musty odor that hinted at the "has been" status of the faded but ornate décor. We peered into the theatre before going backstage. Courtney, an adorable ten-year-old, who still carried some of her childhood chubbiness, and hadn't quite learned to filter her thoughts, blurted out, "Where are all the *people!*?" I laughed out loud but was filled with dismay. The place was empty—except, that is, for the thirteen people who sat scattered about in the large auditorium.

We quickly made our way backstage, and with only moments to spare Phil and I gathered the children around. They found it very funny and were still giggling about the fact there were virtually no people in the audience. After reigning them in a bit, I looked at them, and with all the earnestness I could muster said, "Kids, as you have seen, there are only a few people here tonight, and a whole bunch of empty seats. This is what I want you to do. I want you to look at those empty seats and imagine that *Jesus* is sitting in *every single one* of them. I want you to sing to *Jesus* tonight. Sing your *very best. He* is listening." As I spoke the words, the truth of them was pressed into my own heart. He *was* there, and He expected our very best.

We stood on the stage and gave it our all! The thirteen attendees were so kind and enthusiastic, and blessed us by purchasing over $300 of our CDs at the end of the concert. Most importantly, Jesus was there, His presence was real.

The very next evening we sang to 900 people. Before the concert began, I gathered the children and reminded them that Jesus was here, too! I told them that every person matters to God, and whether there were many or few, we would sing for Jesus and do our best.

One evening sometime later, we ended up at a large venue. We'd been booked at the last minute, and *only* because the promoter was needing another group did she reluctantly agree to "try out" this "new little family." We knew no one...and no one knew us. We were to be singing with other ministry groups who had decades of experience and were well-known and loved by the promoter and the audience. I felt our need for God's help desperately. Everyone was kind, but we felt way out of our comfort zone. We prepared our hearts; Phil and I had prayer and selected the songs we would sing. I gathered the kids around me and told them the story from Luke 14. I said these words: "Kids, tonight we are sitting at the end of the table." I went further and assured them this was actually a *wonderful* place to be. We weren't singing to fulfill any expectations—there were none. We were singing to glorify Jesus, and *hopefully* bring hope and encouragement to every person who was kind enough to listen.

As we sang, God blessed us and His presence filled the building. As we exited the stage at the end of our set, the promoter met me at the bottom of the stairs with tears streaming down her face. I know it wasn't The Collingsworth Family, but the favor and presence of God. We've sung at this same event many times in the ensuing years, but none were more memorable than that first time.

Our kids loved attending the largest annual gospel music event in the US each year, the National Quartet Convention. The first year we actually paid to have our own booth was unforgettable. We sold a grand total of *four CDs* during the week-long event. The kids didn't mind the thousands of people who passed our table without stopping. They were too busy running around gathering autographs from their favorite artists.

These were humbling times of personal growth; of following God, working hard, and learning to leave the results in his hands. I remember coming to the place where I told the Lord that whether we ever sang to more than thirty people, it was okay. There is nothing wrong with success of course. I would be untruthful were I to say I don't enjoy the exciting opportunities God has graciously brought our way. He loves to bless His children, and we should accept His gifts with grateful hearts. However, I do believe that holding loosely to whatever success we may experience is key. I believe true contentment comes when we choose the giver over the gift.

A. W. Tozer wrote so powerfully:

> God may allow His servant to succeed when He has disciplined
> him to a point where he does not have to succeed to be happy. The
> man who is elated by success and is cast down by failure is still a
> carnal man. At best, his fruit will have a worm in it.

On Being Grounded in God

When I was just thirteen, I experienced a crisis in my faith. I was
traveling the country playing piano for a college quartet. I had already attended more church services, heard more sermons, and witnessed more
altar calls than most do in a lifetime. I was serious about my relationship
with Jesus, and He was real to me. I'm not sure why, but there came a
period of time when I found myself doubting that God really loved me.
My parents were all about God's grace, but in my travels I had heard
some preaching that was heavy on law and very light on grace. I was
young and impressionable and became super conscientious, as though
I couldn't quite measure up to the expectations of God and the Bible.
Perhaps it was partially my youth, but in hindsight I believe it was also
an intentional attack of Satan against me. God seemed so far away, and
I couldn't feel His presence as I once had. I felt *especially* that I shouldn't
be up front playing the piano and thus appearing to be an example of a
good Christian young person while I was fighting such internal battles
of my own.

It was during this time that we had a series of special services at our
school. Our special speaker, Rev. Don Myers, came to me one afternoon
and asked if I would be willing to come to the piano during his sermon
and play a song to illustrate a point he would be making. I declined at
first. I was struggling and didn't really want to be up front that day. He
asked again, assuring me it would be okay and that he really wanted me
to play. I reluctantly agreed. He told me he wanted a verse and chorus
of the hymn, "In the Garden." As I sat in my chair waiting for my que,
my heart was pounding, and I had never felt so nervous. It was crazy. I

played piano all the time, but for some reason this was different. I kept repeating the name of the song under my breath for fear I wouldn't remember what to play. I even wrote the title of the song on the palm of my hand in an attempt to remember. As Rev. Myers so eloquently spoke that morning, he impressed upon all of us that God could make a beautiful difference in our lives if only we would give all of ourselves to Him. He began to talk about the piano, and as he did so he walked to the keyboard and began to somewhat awkwardly tap out the melody. After a few lines, he straightened up and addressed the young people who, by the looks on their faces, wondered what he was doing. "Kids, I'm not too impressive, am I? This piano doesn't sound that great with me playing it, does it?" He went on to say, "But there is a young girl here who is a master of this instrument, and I want you to see the difference a "master" can make." With that, he beckoned me forward. I trembled as I slid onto the bench, placed my hands on the keys and...*froze*! My mind was completely blank. I had no idea what I was to play, nor how to play it. The keys seemed foreign to me, as if I'd never played a song in my life. I sat for a moment, a young girl in a crisis. I did the only thing I knew to do: "God, help me!" I prayed. Instantly, I began to play the beautiful chords as the lyrics washed over my heart.

> And He walks with me,
> And He talks with me,
> And He tells me I am His own.
> And the joy we share as we tarry there
> None other has ever known.[8]

There were two profound things that happened as I played. First, God's presence filled the room. My mom was in the audience, and to this day talks about the sweet presence of Jesus. There wasn't a dry eye in the house. And many young people came forward to dedicate all of themselves to God. God's presence and assurance washed over me, too,

8 Charles Austin Miles, *In the Garden*, 1912

as I sat on the bench. I was overwhelmed as the doubts and fears dissipated, never to return. The second thing that happened was this: for the first time in my life I became aware of my gift—*God's gift—the gift* He'd shared with me, for the sake of others. I knew in that moment that I was only a steward of it, and that it was given to me for a purpose greater than myself. It was wonderful, freeing, humbling, and I pray I never forget it.

I have been reminded of this many times. I remember when Phil began pushing me to do more piano solos. One Sunday morning we were singing in Pennsylvania. Phil asked me to play "Amazing Grace." I played, God came down, and the people responded. The Holy Spirit was working through the music and lyrics—it was palpable. The weight of my responsibility settled over me that afternoon. Phil and I were staying that week in a house provided for our family. The kids were small, so in order to be alone I made my way to an attic room. I lay on my face and said, "God, I don't know what happened when I played this morning, but this is your gift. I lay it down and give it back to you again. It is yours! Do with it what you will!" I meant those words then and still do today.

I have been blessed countless times with God's presence and anointing when I play. I don't take it for granted. Early on, the kindness of people, the compliments and praise after a concert, left me feeling self-conscious and troubled. I didn't know how to handle it. I was aware, even then, that I wasn't immune to pride. I enjoyed the praise as anyone would. But I was mindful of the danger of forgetting that I was a steward of a gift. I didn't want to forget that truth.

It was during this time that I heard a sermon preached by a well-known and loved speaker. He told of how he would often receive compliments and pats on the back for his sermons, his preaching style, and effectiveness. He talked about the day he realized his tendency to pride and self-absorption in the midst of all the accolades. He told of how God spoke to him clearly, "These are accolades that people give you, and it's okay to enjoy them….from the platform to your car. And then open your hands and release them back to me because *you can't handle them.*

And it all belongs to me." This impacted me profoundly as a young artist. It helped me to not take myself or the praise of men too seriously. To not internalize the applause. It helped me see my ability for what it was... is—a gift.

In my piano room today I have a trophy case that is full of awards. I don't write this to boast. It's just a reality in my life. I'm grateful for the Dove Award, the Silver Telly Award, the Grammy nomination, and Musician and Mixed Group of the Year Awards. I am so grateful for my many friends who love and believe in me and in the music. But by God's grace, the awards don't define me. I have realized that I mustn't ever become too distracted or impressed by any of those things. I have never forgotten what that speaker said so long ago and have endeavored to implement his strategy for staying grounded. I have practiced giving the awards and praise back to God each time I have received them. I enjoy them, even savor them for a moment—from the stage to the bus. And then...I gladly hand them over to the one who truly deserves honor. I don't ever want to forget that they represent more than hard work; they represent an abundance of grace.

Staying on the Path of Peace

I found some notes from a journal in which I had written some thoughts shared in a sermon by Rev. Daniel Stetler many years ago. He was preaching on the topic of "Peace with God." "Having peace *with* God gives us the peace *of* God," he said. "God's peace is a *directive* peace. He *guides* us with his peace." He went on to admonish us to, "Never move forward or make major decisions if there is a lack of peace."

I recorded these admonitions because I didn't want to forget them. The truth of the message hit Phil and me with tremendous force. It made so much sense. To be honest, in those days as Phil and I were trying to find our place in ministry, we'd gotten ourselves into some uncomfortable situations, too often moving headlong without really pausing to wait on the Lord. I'm thinking specifically of a motorhome we purchased which nearly devastated us financially, an investment house we bought and lost our shirts on, and a couple of ministry positions we accepted based solely on human reasoning. I don't *totally* regret these mistakes, as God redeemed them in our lives, and taught us valuable lessons. But if waiting on the Lord and letting the "peace of God rule" can keep us out of the "woodshed," then I'm all in.

I've learned to allow God's peace to be a directive in my life—not only in the big decisions, but in the little ones as well. There have been countless moments when important decisions about the direction of the CFAM ministry have loomed before us—moments when, even after much prayer and weighing all the facts and details, our decision rested on "do we both feel peace?" God has guided us with His peace time and again.

We've learned that peace is obtained by staying on the path of obedience, by obeying what the word of God says, as well as any specific applications and directives unique to our family. Early in our ministry, Phil and I were faced with a decision that to many others may seem silly or insignificant. And one we've been questioned about countless times over the past twenty years. We decided early on that the CFAM would not sell products on Sundays. Phil and I were both raised in a tradition which emphasised the sacred observance of "The Lord's Day." Sundays were treated as a "different" day. As a rule, we did not buy, sell, or go out to eat on Sunday. It was a day completely set apart from the rest of the week. Sunday was for worship, Christian ministry, rest, and for enjoying family around the dinner table. Even today, on our weekends at home, I cook a big Sunday dinner, and we enjoy the fellowship of our friends and family. It's wonderful!

When Phil and I started this ministry our largest crowds were on Sundays, thus our greatest opportunity for product sales—an indispensable source of our income. We were challenged to know what to do. We took our dilemma to our Tuesday night prayer meeting and asked the Lord what *He* would have us do. We sensed God's direction in the form of a question: "Will you trust me with Sundays?" Then we came up with a solution we both felt peace in implementing. We would allow folks to take our products and leave behind their names and addresses. We refer to this today as our "Sunday Billings." I have been asked dozens of times, "Isn't this legalistic?" I don't think so. It's what God has asked of *us*. We have *peace* about this decision, and that's all that matters. We do not judge or think others must do as we do in any way. And there have been times when we've been overseas, and Sunday billings were impossible. In those instances we have sold our CDs on Sunday.

I specifically struggled with worry. I'm a planner, always organizing and calculating, making double sure things are in order. This no-sales-on-Sunday decision tested my faith like few things had to that point. To pack up and leave a church on Sunday after having watched thousands of dollars of product "vanish" from our tables was a step of faith for me. And I must admit there've been times I've pushed the worry down and pasted on a smile, all the while thinking to myself, *"What if they don't pay!"* I've learned that the peace of obeying is far better than forfeiting peace by doing things my way.

In twenty years of ministry, our rate of pay for our Sunday billings is more than ninety-nine percent! God's people pay their bills. And for those who do not, we leave them in God's hands. Perhaps there are legitimate reasons, and I pray they are blessed by the music anyway.

An unexpected blessing of the Sunday billings is that we now have a database of households that have purchased CFAM product which numbers more than 60,000. We had no idea when we took that step of obedience that we'd gain so much good from it. This database has allowed us to mail product catalogues and send postcards announcing upcoming concerts. This has been an incredible boost to the ministry in countless ways. And God knew this all along!

Personal Peace

Colossians 3:15 has become one of my life verses. It reads, "Let the peace of Christ rule in your hearts, since as members of one body you were called to peace. And be thankful." (NIV)

This truth convicted me deeply during a season of life when the kids, the schedule, the packing, and even my marriage were leaving me anxious, stressed, and anything but peaceful. Though we tried our best to manage the schedule, be home as much as possible, and set some rhythm to our lives, I would often wake up with the demands of the day looming over me like an unscalable mountain. I felt exhausted before my feet ever hit the floor. The Holy Spirit began to summon me, revealing that he had so much more for me than mere survival. He began to show me that I needed to pursue peace in my life. He was faithful to show me my deficiencies and to humble me.

One day I completely lost track of time while spending a grueling day in the schoolroom with the kids, and getting bogged down with the girls and their algebra (which is enough to put even a saint in a bad mood). We were to be on the Eastern Shore of Maryland the following night, and Phil must have gotten concerned and came downstairs to remind me that the bus was pulling out at 5 p.m. I hadn't loaded the bus, there were no clean sheets, or towels, or breakfast foods. I still needed to finish up school for the day, figure out which textbooks we needed to take with us for the weekend, and a million other details. My attitude took a nosedive and, sadly, Phil got a load of my exhaustion and negativity.

I somehow muddled through the next couple hours, got everything completed, and we headed out.

After stopping for supper, the kids headed for their bunks and got settled in for the night. Phil was driving while I sat on the couch with a sigh, thankful for a few minutes to relax, but also feeling troubled in my spirit. My peace was disturbed. The Holy Spirit gently began speaking to me. He helped me to see that if I wanted my children to really believe in the God we sang about, I had to be authentic. Not to be perfect, not to live without mistakes, but to humble myself for the actions and attitudes I had displayed that afternoon.

I made my way to the bunks and began with Brooklyn. She was about thirteen, and I asked her to forgive me for my impatience and the way I had spoken to her father. "Aww mom," she said, "It's okay, you're just tired. You and dad need to get away for a couple of days, and you'll be just fine." I love kids! When I finished apologizing to the children, I felt great...for about three seconds.

"Uh, Kim, you're not done. There's one more person you need to apologize to," I heard that still small voice of the Holy Spirit say. This was difficult, and my pride resisted for a moment. *God, are you sure?* He was. I made my way to the front of the bus and put my arm around my husband and asked him to forgive me. Phil is so gracious and kind, and he assured me that all was well. The peace of God that filled my heart was so wonderful and healing to my spirit.

The next evening, we sang to four hundred women. During the program, I was asked to come back onto the stage and speak for a few moments. I stood before the mic to address the audience, and from the corner of my eye I saw my four children peeking from behind a curtain backstage. They were watching me and listening! The events of the previous evening came before me, and I realized that the words I was preparing to speak would mean little to them were they not reinforced by the way I lived and acted at home. It was sobering. I am reminded of a penetrating message from our friend, Pastor Brent Snook, given not long ago: "The light that shines the farthest shines the brightest at home."

I recently discovered a journal entry from this soul-searching season. It is a bit raw, but it's real and it's where I was living:

> I feel such a need to pursue godliness. To pursue it is to consciously make decisions to respond kindly, act Christlike, to carefully choose my reactions to line up with the way Jesus would act. This is very hard. I tend to be self-centered much of the time. Lord, take that away; help me to be sensitive to your Holy Spirit. I live a fast-paced life, and it is sometimes very easy for me to respond impatiently. Stop me in my tracks. Convict me! Help me to respect and revere your Word and obey it!

The pathway of peace was a path I began to walk with the Lord, even with sometimes faltering steps. As I studied the meaning of "Let the peace of God rule," I learned that to "rule" means to "*preside; to sit as umpire; to govern or control.*" According to the Albert Barnes Commentary, this word "rule" was the same word used in reference to the Olympic games. It meant, to be "a director, or arbiter of the public games; to preside over them and preserve order."

I began to reflect on this, and in my simple way of thinking the Lord began to show me that I needed to let the peace of God "be the umpire," to let the peace of God "call the shots." So when my peace would get disturbed, the Holy spirit would say to me, "Fix it now! Go back and apologize. Make it right, now." This is how my peace is restored. I have found that humble pie is most bitter going down, but as it settles, it is incredibly sweet. And that humility trumps being "right," *every single time.*

This matter of allowing the peace of God to rule in my heart was serious. I needed to be attentive to any actions, words, or attitudes which disturbed my peace, and to make whatever adjustments needed for peace to be restored. I needed to allow divine peace to govern my words, responses, and reactions.

I began to understand that it wasn't life's stresses, or busyness, or persistent travel that destroyed my peace. These were the tangible realities of life, but in every difficulty I faced there were deeper spiritual realities I needed to be aware of. Jesus said in John 10:10, "The thief comes only to steal and kill and destroy." Satan was using *these* things to rob me of the promise of Jesus, who went on to say, " I have come that they may have life, and have it to the full."

As I continued my study, I discovered I Peter 5:8, which reads, "Be alert and of a sober mind. Your enemy the devil prowls around like a roaring lion looking for someone to devour. Resist him, standing firm in the faith..."

I began to see that I needed to be intentional about "resisting" Satan and his attempts to rob me of my peace and joy. One of the ways I did this was to identify those weak areas in my life which tempted me toward anxiety. I began to pay attention to my most susceptible moments.

When I am exhausted, I have learned to go to sleep and to postpone any important discussions or concerns I may have. For me, exhaustion paired with problem solving results in negativity, too many words, the wrong words, and the destruction of peace.

Phil came into the kitchen one evening and began a discussion concerning a certain matter. He made a statement that I thought he misquoted. I called him on it, and he disagreed with me. As I became more assertive in my position, Phil smiled, walked over to me, put his arms around me and whispered, "Babe, your peace is getting disturbed." He was right. I laughed and let it go.

The Word of God commands us to, "Put on the full armor of God, so that you can take your stand against the devil's schemes. For our struggle is not against flesh and blood, but against the rulers, against the authorities, against the powers of this dark world and against the spiritual forces of evil in the heavenly realms" (Ephesians 6:11-12).

This passage goes on to describe the armor as the belt of truth, the breastplate of righteousness, shoes that are fitted with the Gospel of *peace*, the shield of faith, the helmet of salvation, and the sword of the Spirit which is the *Word of God*.

I wrote this passage in my journal with the following note:

> Satan is going to fight! Satan does roam like a roaring lion seeking whom he may devour. But if we are constantly alert—and understand that by using God's Word as a weapon, we can overcome his attacks on us. We must get into God's Word and get God's Word into us! This is our defense! God help me to be self-controlled and alert, taking on the whole armor of God!

Saturating our minds with God's truth is a powerful way to stay on the path of peace.

A few years ago, I sat and listened as Dr. David Jeremiah preached a powerful message on this topic. I grabbed a pen and wrote his words in the back of my Bible. This powerful thought has impacted my life.

> "The Holy Spirit is the software to your hard drive. When we
> memorize Scripture and put it on our hard drive, the Holy Spirit
> brings his Word up on the screen of our lives. If we have nothing
> on our hard drive, we give the Holy Spirit very little to work with."

I internalized this truth, and it was soon put to the test. I was having a
conversation with an individual when a very hurtful statement was made
about someone I happen to care about a great deal. Indignation bubbled
to the surface, and I opened my mouth to deliver a sharp, well-deserved
rebuke.

The words I so badly wanted to speak were stopped short, when
a passage I had been studying flashed up on the screen of my mind.
Proverbs 19:11 admonishes: "A person's wisdom yields patience; it is to
one's glory to overlook an offense."

I paused, still wanting to vent my anger, but I heard the Holy Spirit
gently say, "Kim, do you want to be wise? Or do you want to be bitter?"
I kept my mouth shut! I thank him for his faithfulness to me in that moment. The Word of God is powerful, and speaks to all of life.

I read that only twenty-nine percent of Christians read the Bible daily. It is sobering to think that seventy-one percent of believers are going
to the wrong places for life's answers.

When we stumble through life, speaking, acting, and responding
apart from the wisdom found in the Word of God, we will surely stray
from enjoying God's peace.

The Bible is so full of wonderful truth on this matter of peace and
the rewards that pursuing peace yields to the believer. I will share a few
of my favorites:

> "Make every effort to live in peace with everyone and to be holy"
> (Hebrews 12:14).

> "Peacemakers who sow in peace reap a harvest of righteousness"
> (James 3:18).

> "Those who promote peace love joy" (Proverbs 12:20b).

"How good and pleasant it is when God's people live together in unity! For there the Lord bestows his blessing, even life forevermore" (Psalm 133:1,3b).

"Thou will keep him in perfect peace, whose mind is stayed on thee: because he trusteth in thee" (Isaiah 26:3, KJV).

And then there are these beautiful words of Jesus:

"Peace I leave with you; my peace I give you. I do not give to you as the world gives. Do not let your hearts be troubled and do not be afraid" (John 14:27).

Joyce Meyer once said, "The Word of God will set you free, but only if applied." I believe it is also true that, "The Word of God will bring you peace, but only if applied."

9

WHEN GOD OPENS THE DOOR

Wherever you are,
Wherever you're going,
God is right there beside you,
Seeing and knowing.[9]

The Fall of 2003 was an exciting time for us. We were a little more than three years into this new adventure God had called us to. We were singing nearly every weekend and enjoying God's blessing. Our lives hummed along to the rhythm of raising children, homeschooling, practice time, and busy weekends on the road. We were traveling in a twelve-passenger van, and pulling a trailer. We pinched pennies, packed lunches, and prayed for good prices on fuel!

We were quite shocked when we received a phone call from someone at the INSP Television Network, asking us if they could air our first video recording (recorded the previous year), "One Special Evening."

The recording of that project at Calvary Baptist Church in Covington, Kentucky, had been such a wonderful event. The audience was enthusiastic and was made up of not only the church members, but also, many of our own family members and friends had joined to celebrate the evening with us. We assembled a choir by sending out invitations to people

9 The Collingsworth Family, *Wherever You Are*, track #7, That Day is Coming, Stowtown Records, 2015, CD

whom we knew could sing. This included friends, family, and some of Phil's college classmates. The Music Pastor from the church, Mr. Dave Ellington, agreed to conduct the choir, and they backed us up on several songs. The kids were so little and a bit nervous about being on camera. At twelve years old, Brooklyn sang the third part on the songs we had recorded earlier with my sister Becky, and although her voice was young and a bit timid, she nailed every note.

We still aren't sure how this video recording landed in the hands of the folks at INSP, but when they asked if they could air it and explained there would be no charge for doing so, we were delighted. If you go to INSP network today, you will find old westerns and other clean TV shows, but in 2003, it was strictly Christian programming.

We had no idea what the outcome of this television airing would be, but I won't forget what happened the morning after our video aired on television.

I woke up early and heard the phone ringing in the office. I headed downstairs, still in my pajamas, and picked up the phone. I didn't make it *back* upstairs until late in the evening. Each time I put the phone down, it rang again. I took phone orders and information for concert requests all day long. We had a part-time office manager at the time, and between Sherilyn and me, we took almost ninety requests for concerts within the first week!

We were totally overwhelmed. Phil reached out to Michael Davis, an established booking agent in the gospel music industry, within that week to ask for help. Though I was a bit reluctant about this at first, and was afraid of losing that personal touch in the office, we desperately needed assistance. We had no infrastructure in place to handle this demand. We had reached out to this agency previously but had been turned down, as our family wasn't known, and really didn't have much to offer an agent in terms of demand.

When Phil told Michael Davis our need, he pulled our DVD from the closet where he had placed it unopened a year earlier and played it before calling us back and accepting the CFAM. What a relief! He was invaluable to our family, and took over all the booking details for us.

Sharing Christmas with our troops

This was a crazy time. So much was happening. At the time of the airing of our DVD, we were also preparing to go to Pristina, Kosovo (at the request of the Department of Defense), to sing for the US troops, and civilians, on two different military bases. We were to perform two Christmas concerts on Christmas Eve and Christmas Day of 2003.

We were excited but nervous. We were pros at the rigors of travel but *not* outside the USA. It was a whirlwind of a week. We left the USA on December 22, and spent an unexpected night in Paris after missing our connection. It was hectic, trying to figure out what to do with our sixteen large cases of sound and video equipment, but we ended up renting a hotel room at the airport just to store it all.

Our plane landed in Macedonia where, after stepping onto the tarmac, we spotted my brother Brian (serving on the base) through a plexiglass window. He looked as if he would burst with excitement. It was freezing cold while we stood in a line surrounded by heavy security, including guards with assault rifles. It was hardly a convenient time for five-year old Olivia to tug at my skirt with a desperate, "Mommy, I've got to *go!*' We found the bathroom, but Olivia had a meltdown when she saw the eastern style "squat toilet" (yep, that's what they call them)! I coaxed her along, and we both survived (barely) her first encounter with a non-western facility.

After being loaded onto a military transport, we set out for our trip to the base. I've heard missionaries tell of these dangerous trips on treacherous roads, but I never thought I'd experience them myself. We sat shivering from the cold on a bus that had no heat, as our driver traversed snow-covered, slippery roads with very little visibility. We were thankful for the military escort both in front and behind. Sometime after 8 p.m. we arrived at Camp Bondsteel.

Over the next two days, we had the honor of bringing a little Christmas cheer to the men and women who sacrifice everything to ensure peace, comfort, and freedom for the rest of us. We spoke with so many of them, heard their stories, and gave and received heartfelt hugs from moms, dads, sons, and daughters. I know they missed their families so much, and many were especially drawn to five-year-old Olivia. And when we played *our* Christmas surprise for them, a prerecorded video that Phil had worked hard to obtain of their wives, husbands, and children giving their love and Christmas greetings from back home, I cried right along with the brave men and women who sat wiping away tears.

Most importantly, we shared the simple Gospel through the telling of the Christmas story. It was a once in a lifetime, unforgettable kind of Christmas.

Grand Cayman

After recovering from our Christmas tour and trip to Kosovo, we hopped on another plane and headed for Grand Cayman. The kids were wowed when a limousine picked us up and took us to our hotel. It was a privilege to sing for Lorna Blackman, the principal of a large public school on the island. We were also hosted by missionaries, John and Betty Case, who took us on a tour, showing us the beautiful beaches and their favorite places. Phil and I took an afternoon to enjoy the beach with the kids, and then we sang to a super enthusiastic crowd in a packed out gymnasium. God's presence was in the room, and the worship was heartfelt and lively.

The ministry was gaining momentum as God began opening new doors. INSP aired the DVD from our trip to Kosovo, "Christmas in Kosovo," and heeding some good counsel, we hired an independent call center to set up an 800-number to take our calls and orders after the airing. Michael Davis was now handling all the booking and setting up the logistics of each date.

Though we had a part-time office manager, we often had to solicit help from the kids to send out mailings in those days. They were great sports. I found the following entry, and remember this evening well.

> The girls, Phil, and I stayed up until 2 a.m. folding advertisements and putting labels on our new recording. We had about 900 names and churches. Wow! What a big job, but so much fun!

It was exciting, but daunting, when the churches and auditoriums began filling up. We were singing to packed-out buildings, and the weight and responsibility of this was equal to the joy. We knew we weren't adequate in our own strength, and that apart from the Holy Spirit, we couldn't be trusted with this. We felt our desperate need. The kids were small and cute—but this wasn't enough. We knew we had to depend upon God every single time we stood to sing, and though the children were still maturing musically, we marveled when his presence would come and melt hearts as they sang simple truths—truths such as this one, penned by Joel Hemphill:

> We have a heavenly Father above,
> With eyes full of mercy, and a heart full of love;
> He really cares when your head is bowed low,
> Consider the lilies and then you will know.[10]

Phil was quite taken back when asked by a well-meaning man, "What's your *shtick*?" We didn't know what he meant. What we *knew* was that, in Phil's words, "We were just a little family trying to sing well, pray, and minister through the help of the Holy Spirit. We *knew* we were called to this work, and that any success was a blessing from the Lord."

In 2005, I received a phone call from Roger Bennet, owner of Legacy Five, and former pianist for the Cathedral Quartet. I had admired Roger and his piano playing for years but had never had the privilege of meeting him. He invited me to join him and others at his annual "Roger Bennett's

---

10 The Collingsworth Family, *Consider the Lilies*, track #8, Lifting Our Voices, P&KC Music, 2000, CD

Parade of Pianos," which took place in Louisville, Kentucky each year at the National Quartet Convention.

According to Roger, he had been pestered for several years by people who wanted him to invite me to the Parade of Pianos showcase. I guess I have faithful and loyal friends. Perhaps he grew weary of hearing my name and decided to contact me.

It was an honor to share the stage with Roger and other talented piano players for an afternoon. I sat surrounded by men and must admit that it was a bit unsettling. The floor length dress I had chosen to wear for the occasion hid my shaking legs as I waited my turn.

My name was called and I made my way to the bench and waited for the track. I breathed a prayer and began to play as the lyrics to "How Great Thou Art" permeated my being. My nerves calmed as I leaned into the keys, giving my *all* in an effort to communicate the truth of those words through music. I felt God's thumb in my back, and His presence overwhelmed me as I played. I was made aware, once again, that it was *His* gift, and that He was using it, *and* me, as a conduit of His grace. What a wonderful awareness.

I stood for four hours that afternoon, and greeted hundreds and hundreds of people. I heard their stories and saw their tears flow as they shared their joys and sorrows, and testimonies of the faithfulness of God. I was humbled when they expressed how they had experienced God's presence as I played. I thanked them, as I should have, but I knew it really wasn't about me. It must never be. It's all about *Him*! I recorded very simply in my journal that evening:

God helped me tremendously, and I felt His presence.

We connected that week with so many who would be instrumental in helping the CFAM in new ways. We were already working part time with Wayne Haun, a wonderful orchestrater who went on to become our producer for thirteen years. We met those who would go on to write many songs for our family: Joel Lindsey ("Ever Faithful", "The Lamb", and others), Tom and Rebecca Peck ("Blessed be the Lamb"), and Gerald Crabb ("I Can Trust Jesus"). I know that God often works through His people and uses all our gifts together to advance His Kingdom in this world.

The Music Hall "Miracle"

Phil has always been "the man with a plan." This is his gift, and one of the things I love about him, though there have been moments when these plans have driven me to the brink of *insanity*! My careful, methodical approach to life bears a striking contrast to Phil's larger-than-life visions of "what might be," and his readiness to take risks.

In 2008, we planned to record two live videos in one evening. This time we would use the lovely Memorial Hall Performing Arts Center in downtown Cincinnati, Ohio, a historic building which features marble staircases adorned with intricate wrought iron leading to the 556 seat proscenium theater. It is exquisitely adorned with decorative murals and Tiffany Chandeliers. It is elegant, yet intimate—just the "feel" we were seeking for the event.

The plan was to give free tickets to ensure filling the building. This worked well, and every seat was reserved. There were people who had flown in for the event and were staying in town.

On the morning of the concert, March 8, 2008, I woke up and turned on the news, and to my horror saw that Cincinnati was in for a blizzard. I peered out the window and, sure enough, the beginning of what would be seventeen inches of snow was falling from the skies in a cold, white torrent. Phil scrambled, making phone calls, and letting our producer and TV trucks know that we had to cancel. They were already in Cincinnati, and Phil urged them to get out of town immediately if they hoped to get back to Phoenix. It was surreal; the months of planning, the advertising, the financial commitments we had made—all out the window, just like that. I couldn't help but breathe, *God, what are you doing?*

Phil wasn't deterred. He just set about working on "Plan B." I stood

around and wrung my hands for a few days, while Phil checked dates
and venues in an effort to reschedule as soon as possible. We would not
be able to reserve Memorial Hall. They had no open dates. There was,
however, one option to be explored.

We would be home for the week of April 17, as this was an annual church convention we attended each year. The convention, held in
Dayton, Ohio, ended on Thursday night, the 18th. We had Friday night,
the 19th, available, and thought perhaps we could pull some attendees who were already in town for the convention, which hosted several
thousand people.

Now for the venue. Phil discovered that the Cincinnati Music Hall
was available for that date. I was incredulous when he mentioned it to
me. While Music Hall is considered one of the best and most beautiful concert theatres in the world—with impeccable acoustics, glittering
chandeliers, and old-world ambience—I questioned Phil's judgment for
thinking we could *actually* pull off Music Hall.

Phil made an appointment to view the place, and coaxed me into
going along. I stood on the stage and looked out over the vast auditorium while hot tears of frustration, unbelief, and resistance filled my eyes
and threatened to spill over. *We could never fill even a third of this building,* I thought. I tentatively asked the manager, "Could you black out the
third gallery?" she assured me that she could. "What about the second
gallery?" I then asked if we could black out part of the main floor. She
hesitated, but said that perhaps she could do this. I'm sure she thought
we were crazy, and wondered why we were even bothering if our crowd
would be that small.

Phil and I had a rather "intense conversation" on the drive home. He
was adamant that he felt this was God's will. "Kim, we need to do this!"
he assured me. As I pondered his plan to rent this audacious building,
give away free tickets, and record two videos in one night, I reminded
him that there was a fine line between "God's will" and *stupidity,* and I
was pretty sure he was about to cross that line.

Later that evening, I acquiesced and told Phil to do what he felt best. And then I got busy worrying. Fear crept in and hovered over me for days.

Sometimes God unlocks a door and beckons for us to try the knob, but we hesitate and allow fear to hold us back. In this instance, God was using my husband's forward thinking and clear vision to help us through that door, but my fear and unbelief were leaving me behind in the process.

I found the following journal entry from March 21, 2008, to be interesting:

> Proverbs 21:20, "The wise have wealth and luxury, but fools spend whatever they get" (NLT).

My thought when I read this verse was sanctimonious and a little proud: *Oh, yes Lord, Phil is absolutely crazy and he's devouring all we have!* I continued to read and write:

> Proverbs 21:23, "Those who guard their mouths and their tongues keep themselves from calamity."

Ouch Lord, you're talking about me here!

I winced as I fell from my high horse. The message was loud and clear!

I continued journaling:

> Proverbs 21:30-31, This is my word for the day! "There is no wisdom, no insight, no plan that can succeed against the Lord. The horse is made ready for the day of battle, but victory rests with the Lord."
>
> Awoke this morning with fear and heaviness all over me. It was so real I could almost touch it. These two verses are for me today. "Victory rests with the Lord!" We will prepare the horse for battle and leave the rest to God. That is a sure and safe place to live!

At this point, despite my tendency to fear, I went to Phil and stated, "Phil, I'm on board."

This entry was added to every few days until the day of the Music Hall taping:

> Phil put the announcement on our website on Wednesday 3/19/08 at around 6 p.m. By 7:15 p.m. we had 320 tickets reserved. Phil and I went out to Olive Garden for supper and were gone for three hours. By the time we arrived home we were up to 630 reservations. By last night we were over 1,400, and by 2 p.m. Friday, 3/21/08, we were sitting at 1,533 reserved seats. I wish we could have 2,300 people. That would be awesome. Victory rests with the Lord! This is absolute security!
>
> Today is Tuesday 3/25/08 and we're at 1,885.
>
> 4/5/08, 2,888.
>
> 4/19/08, ended up with well over 3,300 in the audience.

All tickets were given for free, and between the free-will offering and product sales, the cost of the entire event and the two video projects was covered by the end of the night.

Victory does, indeed, rest with the Lord!

Bill and Gloria Gaither

The smooth harmonies of Bill, Gloria, and Danny Gaither had been the soundtrack of my childhood. I still remember the long console stereo system with the red velvet speaker covers we had. Mom would play Gaither albums by the hour, and my siblings and I often sang along. The Keaton Trio sang Gaither songs such as "Joy in the Camp," and others.

Throughout 2007-2008, The Collingsworth Family was invited to sing some dates with Bill and Gloria and their Homecoming team. We made wonderful friends, and enjoyed singing with other artists to packed out arenas. I loved watching Bill orchestrate each concert. He is a master, and he instinctively knew how to craft the program. Sometimes he'd change course on a dime, and you had to be ready.

Bill sometimes ended these concert evenings with an old Gaither classic. It was always quite the moment when he would bring Gloria out onto the stage and talk his way into that familiar verse:

> How sweet to hold a newborn baby,
> And feel the pride and joy he gives,
> But greater still, the calm assurance
> This child can face uncertain days, because He lives.[11]

The first time Bill beckoned me to the piano bench at the beginning of this song, it was kind of surreal. I sat, following the arrangement and key changes as the Gaither Vocal Band ministered those powerful words.

As I played, I envisioned myself—a small girl dancing around the coffee table as a *much younger* Bill Gaither sang, "Noah Found Grace in the Eyes of the Lord." I couldn't help but wonder, *How is it that I'm here, now, playing this music for Bill Gaither?*

In 2009 our family traveled with Gaithers and the Homecoming team, singing thirty-five dates across the US. This gave us a much broader audience, and we met thousands of new friends, which opened more doors for the CFAM. Our kids made good friends and enjoyed hanging out with the children of the other artists on tour. There was fun camaraderie among all of us, which made the tour enjoyable. And there were powerful moments as we sang and worshipped together night after night.

We found Bill and Gloria to be warm, kind, and gracious people. While singing at Gaither Fest in Myrtle Beach one year, Bill popped on the bus one day without bothering to knock. I looked down the hall, and there he was with a smile and a "What's going on?" He plopped down on the couch, and we chatted for the next twenty minutes. And Olivia remembers well the "field trip" she enjoyed with her friend Madeline (Bill and Gloria's granddaughter) and Gloria. They visited the Dutch Village in Holland, Michigan, where she bought Olivia a pair of wooden shoes and treated the kids to lunch and ice cream.

---

11 Gaither Music, *Because He Lives,* Words and Music by William J & Gloria Gaither, 1971

Our family was invited to sing with the Homecoming team at the Billy Graham Library. The singing took place in a large tent and was to be a special two-part Homecoming video, honoring the life and legacy of the Rev. Billy Graham.

Bill Gaither had requested that we sing our new song, "The Blood of Jesus." CFAM was prepared, but the morning of the taping I came down with a terrible cough and cold, and lost my voice. I was concerned, as I solo on the verses to this song. We went to the taping, which was an all-day event with around 100 artists. It was an unforgettable day, partly because of the terrible rain storm which threatened to flood the tent. Thankfully, the storm passed, and we continued. I took tiny sips of cough syrup as we waited our turn. I was so grateful for The Hayes Family, seated just behind me, who knew of my predicament and prayed for me throughout the evening. When The Collingsworth Family stood to sing, my voice was strong and clear. It was a miracle for sure.

The highlight of that day, for me, was when George Beverly Shea and Cliff Barrows were ushered out onto the stage. The impromptu sing-along, with Cliff Barrows leading us in "Sweet, Sweet Spirit." was a moment I won't soon forget. I stood thinking about the lives of Billy Graham, George Shea, and Cliff Barrows, and of their impact on the world. I thought of the hundreds of thousands of lives that had been changed through the ministry of these men. What an honor to have been a part of that day.

In 2014, we were surprised and delighted to receive a personal letter from Cliff Barrows, requesting that The Collingsworth Family sing for his retirement celebration. We did so *gladly*, and I count it as a cherished privilege of a lifetime.

Our Gaither connection opened up an opportunity to go with other groups to Sweden and Norway. We were a little puzzled as to how this would work, given the language barrier. When we stepped onto the stage, and our track to "God is in the Shadows" began, the place erupted in applause. It dawned on me that Bill's Homecoming videos had paved the way, and that these people already knew our music. And the sweet presence of the Holy Spirit cannot be overstated. It is universal and powerful in any language or culture where His name is being lifted up.

Greeting our Scandinavian brothers and sisters after each concert was a beautiful experience. They clasped our hands, and their tears and smiles conveyed more than words ever could have.

Things were moving, new opportunities were abounding, and I would write during a ten-day Florida tour:

> We have had wonderful services on this tour. Great spirit, offerings, and sales. Thank the Lord.
>
> I feel such a need to pray tonight for some reason. We've seen such amazing growth in this ministry. I don't want to ever forget where it has come from. It has been God completely!

The more the CFAM ministry grew and expanded, the more I felt my need. I would write:

> It's only because of the blessing of the Lord. We can't afford to lose it in any way. The only way to keep His blessing, is to stay on our knees! We need God so desperately!

We were reminded over and again of the importance of keeping the nucleus of our lives in order—God, our marriage, our children, and their changing needs—no matter how busy and exciting the ministry was becoming. God had interesting ways of keeping us focused on prayer and dependence upon Him.

Wake Up Call

In the midst of the growing pulse of momentum in the ministry, I recorded the following journal entry:

> We sang tonight in Ashland, Ohio. It was a horrible night. Hardly anyone showed up. There were one hundred thirty people seated in an eleven hundred seat auditorium.
>
> We talked about it afterwards as a family. We felt like it was good for us. We've been having such wonderful services and

excellent product sales and great offerings. I think the Lord was reminding us that we need to count our blessings, and to never take for granted what he is doing in and through our lives.

It made us all want to get on our knees and stay there. Thank the Lord for these reminders. I don't ever want to get to the place where we think we're "somebody's." We are "nobody's."

The Lord will let us remember that!

Phil and I tried to be intentional about letting the kids in on our prayer time for the ministry. We talked openly with them about the spiritual aspect of our work, sometimes wondering if they "got it." After one very difficult concert, I wondered no more.

It was an unusually busy season; we were exhausted and in much need of rest. Things were hectic, and we had missed group prayer several nights in a row due to a very tight time schedule. God is so gracious, and I don't want to sound legalistic, but we *were* powering on in the flesh.

We sang one evening to a full house, our voices strong but our "vessels" empty. We made it through but left the building feeling defeated and exhausted. (There is nothing more tiring than attempting to do God's work in one's own strength). Courtney, a teenager then, climbed onto the bus and stood at the front and announced what I already knew: "Guys, that was the *worst* concert we have *ever* had!" She continued, "We have *not* been praying like we should, and we are *not* singing *another* note until we *get on our knees*! We need God's help!" We all agreed with her, and I said to Phil later in the privacy of our room, "Phil, she is saying to us what we have always said to her." It was humbling...in a wonderful way! Our kids *did* understand the role and importance of the Holy Spirit and our dependence upon him.

I wrote in my journal after meditating on I Peter 1:24-25, which reads, "For, all people are like grass, and all their glory is like the flowers of the field; the grass withers and the flowers fall, but the word of the Lord endures forever."

This is a right perspective. We are nothing outside of God's grace. We should be lifting Jesus up to everyone and humbling ourselves before God. I am nothing without God's blessing and grace in my life. I am here for a season and then gone. But God and His word remain forever.

New places, new friends

Perhaps it was the exposure from the Gaither's that brought the call from First Baptist Atlanta, and Dr. Charles Stanley, in 2011. We sang a total of ten songs in two services on a Sunday morning before Dr. Stanley preached the morning message. These were recorded to be played on the In Touch television program, which airs to millions of viewers around the world each week. We didn't have the privilege of meeting Dr. Stanley until the following year, when we were invited back to sing for his eightieth birthday celebration. We have since provided music, along with others, on multiple In Touch cruises to Alaska. Dr. Stanley would often stop by our table at dinner and tease the CFAM about taking up so much space in the dining room. He is a most gracious man. My most memorable event, however, was the In Touch Christmas Special for which we sang in 2015.

We traveled to Helena, Georgia, where the event was to be filmed in a small, white country church built in the 1860's. It was tucked away on a large plantation and had been the place of worship for the folks who had lived there long ago. It was beautifully decorated with lights, trees, poinsettias, and glittering wreaths. We had been given instructions on the types and colors of clothing we were to wear, and the music we were to sing. We were prepared and ready to go.

The evening before the event, we met with a small team of producers from In Touch for last minute instructions. When the man in charge began inquiring about songs that were not on our list to sing, I was caught off guard. And when he went on to request songs we had never sung together, I swallowed, and told him that we would need an hour in the chapel ahead of time, but that we'd be ready. As I spoke, I was frantically arranging music in my head and picking out parts and key changes. We hurried to the small chapel where we spent an hour practicing *new* music for a television special that would be taped the following day and shown to millions of people around the world. It was a bit nerve-wracking, and I instructed the kids, *"Put it to memory!"* And that was that! We sang the next evening to an audience of about forty people with Dr. Stanley on the front row. He then delivered a beautiful Christmas message. It was an honor to be there.

Something I've never shared, but still makes me laugh, also happened just before the taping.

We are accustomed to the necessity of stage make-up, especially when being videoed. In Touch had their own make-up artist, who skillfully made us all up for the video shoot. She suggested that I wear some... fake eyelashes! I politely declined, but she wasn't having it. She pressed me, telling me how nice they would look on camera, and that I needed these to complete my "look." I didn't want to be rude, so I finally told her she could try them... *with* the caveat that if I didn't like them, they were coming off. When she handed me the mirror, I took one look, and resolutely stated, "Nope, this just isn't me! I'll never be able to concentrate on the music with these things on." Besides, I wasn't too keen on changing my look for this taping that was to be aired around the world. I had to be on my game. She was disappointed, but we had a good laugh, and off they came.

We have been astounded and grateful for the interesting places God has led in the past twenty years. I wrote in my journal several years ago:

> When God calls you, He will open the doors, make the connections, and provide the resources. All that He asks of you is a life that is consecrated to doing His will.

I will say here with certainty, that each of us—me, you, and anyone who bears the name Christ, has a work to do for the Lord. And when we follow Him, He will open unique and redemptive doors for us to walk through. And you can be sure that yours will be suited just for you, and mine for me. We are all valued and needed in His kingdom.

In 2014, We were privileged to be invited by Dr. David Jeremiah to Shadow Mountain Community Church, in San Diego, California. There was a wonderful spirit of worship, and the congregation was responsive and enthusiastic. Dr. Jeremiah's ministry continues to be a blessing to our family, and he has become a good friend. When he invited us to accompany director, Tobin Davis, and the Shadow Mountain choir and orchestra as special guests at Carnegie Hall in 2017, we were excited.

We met up in New York City, where, the night before Carnegie Hall, we participated in a flash mob in Times Square, singing "God Bless America" with the choir. It was an unforgettable moment.

Our entire family enjoyed Carnegie Hall. The kids perused the walls bearing the signatures of all the famed musicians who have played in this premiere concert hall. We sang several songs, and I played "Battle Hymn of the Republic" with the full Shadow Mountain Orchestra. I let the music wrap me in its embrace in that beautiful and historical setting, as I thanked God for this opportunity—for allowing me to share his gift in this place.

In July 2018, Phil, once again, began to envision something new for the CFAM. He called a team meeting and challenged us to think about what a three-day worship event, hosted by the CFAM, might look like. Together, we visualized a welcoming venue, good music with an emphasis on worship, and anointed speakers.

This was the birth of "Inspiration Encounter," with the first event held October, 2019, at the Answers in Genesis Performing Arts Center in Williamsburg, Kentucky. Our friend, Ken Ham, and his team, are wonderful to work with, and God is blessing this new ministry.

One of the highlights of our first "IE" weekend was hosting Carol Cymbala and the Brooklyn Tabernacle Choir. With the help of Christian Healthcare Ministries, we flew 206 members from New York City to Cincinnati for the event! They performed a beautiful Friday night concert and brought the house down. We were so grateful for their willingness to share their ministry with us. When Phil asked about the food preferences for the choir, they only had one request. "Could we please go to Cracker Barrel?" I guess Cracker Barrel isn't too much of a "thing" in Brooklyn, New York.

———————

Phil and I had the unexpected privilege of meeting Pastor Jim Cymbala in 2013, while we celebrated our wedding anniversary in New York City. After a fun weekend of seeing the sights of the city, we decided to attend the Brooklyn Tabernacle Church on Sunday morning. We had, like many, heard of the Brooklyn Tabernacle, and had enjoyed the choir, and had read after Pastor Cymbala for many years. When our friend, TaRanda Green (who often sang with the choir), learned we were coming, she reserved seats in the fifth row for us. It was a wonderful service, and both Phil and I wept our way through the worship and the sermon. God's presence was near, and we were ministered to in a powerful way.

Afterwards, we exited the building with masses of people and were preparing to catch a cab back to our hotel, when my phone rang. It was TaRanda. "Where are you? Pastor Cymbala is waiting to meet you in his office." I insistently declined, but TaRanda wouldn't hear of it. I found out later it is common for him to meet guests. He's just that kind of man.

Phil and I made our way to the office where we sat and talked with him for some time. He asked about our work, and when we told him we were gospel music singers, he seemed genuinely interested. He asked if we would send him some of our music. I was embarrassed to do so, but as soon as we arrived home, Phil sent the CDs in the mail.

This began a wonderful relationship with the Brooklyn Tabernacle, with Pastor Jim Cymbala, and with his wife, Carol. When we sing at the Brooklyn Tabernacle, I feel right at home. The emphasis on prayer, and the necessity of the Holy Spirit, is so refreshing. God's presence is welcome in that place, and I've found that He loves to be where He's welcomed. Our prayer times in Pastor Cymbala's office are always meaningful and heartfelt. He and Carol, and the whole team at Brooklyn Tabernacle, hold a special place in our hearts.

We are blessed, and I am utterly grateful to God.

A journal entry from 2018, says it best:

> Sometimes I almost pinch myself at the opportunities afforded our family. It is only God Almighty who could make all of this happen. Lord, your favor is humbling. Help us to always walk in a manner worthy of the calling you have bestowed upon us. Keep us on our toes. Keep us in the center of your perfect will.

10

TALES YOU WON'T HEAR FROM THE STAGE

I like a good story, well told.
That is the reason I am sometimes forced
to tell them myself.
—Mark Twain

When God provided a bus for the CFAM in 2005, I was ecstatic. That first weekend out, I thanked the Lord under my breath as I placed the children's clothes, pajamas, and shoes into their assigned spaces. I could hardly imagine that we wouldn't be driving late into the night looking for hotels, and having to drag all of our belongings inside. Tucking the children into their bunks and knowing they would be getting a full night of sleep was such a relief.

A bus allowed us to go from being a regional group, or having to carefully schedule our concerts within reasonable driving distances, to more of a national concert ministry. Phil and I were young, and perhaps didn't think this through, but there *was* one small issue that posed a bit of a problem. We didn't have a bus driver. Phil sometimes overestimated his youth and ability by doing all the driving himself. It was grueling some weekends. But I never considered there being another option. That is, until one early morning when my sleep in the back room was interrupted.

We had finished a three-hour concert and loaded up the bus. Phil and Phillip did most of the tear down and loading—exhausting work. We needed to drive well into the early morning hours in order to be close enough to the venue for the following night's concert. I was awakened by the phone next to our bed in the back room. It was Phil. "Kim, I'm in trouble. I *cannot* stay awake, and I'm afraid I'm going to kill us all if I keep driving. But we can't stop or we won't make it to our next venue in time." I was silent on my end of the phone as an alarm began going off somewhere in my brain. I knew where this conversation was going. "Kim...you're going to have to drive," He continued. I protested, telling him that it was impossible. Although I had driven a large truck and fifth-wheel trailer...*once* in the past, there was no way I could drive this forty-five-foot machine. Phil was adamant that I was the only hope of us arriving on time for our next concert.

I sat on the side of the bed gathering my thoughts, whispered a prayer, and made my way to the front of the bus. Phil gave me a few pointers and a thirty-second tutorial on how and when to use the transmission retarder. I got into the driver's seat, and before I could protest, Phil, due to complete exhaustion, had disappeared into the back of the bus, leaving me all alone. With a deep breath and a whispered prayer, I eased out onto the interstate. I gained some speed, and my anxiety eased. Ten minutes later, however, I was in full-blown construction with concrete lane dividers on one side of me, and all sorts of construction equipment on the other. I sat straight up, gripping the wheel with both hands—too terrified to call Phil—and wondering how "bus driver" had gotten into my job description. I somehow made it through my "maiden" night as a CFAM chauffeur, and went on to become quite comfortable in the driver's seat. For years afterwards, Phil and I shared the driving. It certainly wasn't my favorite thing to do, but it felt good to be able to help out in this way. We were a team in every single part of this ministry.

Phil and I developed our own unique methods for staying awake on those long, overnight drives. Phil loved listening to preachers, and I'd often hear him yelling his agreement or laughing loudly with the likes of T.

D. Jakes and others. For me, the deep quiet of the night and good coffee was soothing, and just what I needed after a busy day.

Countless times, I've pulled into Wal-Mart parking lots anywhere between 4 a.m. and 7 a.m. with a sigh of relief. After making sure the bus was level and the generator on, I'd leave my post, pull the curtain closed behind the driver's seat, and make for the back bedroom, feeling safe, happy, and at home, knowing the kids and Phil were sleeping soundly. Soon I would be too! All seemed well with the world, and I can honestly say those were some of the best "nights" of sleep I've ever had.

Those middle of the night forays into Wal-Mart parking lots didn't always end well. Although it's common for truckers or buses to do this, we've been awakened countless times by fierce banging on the bus, and a manager barking, "You can't park here!" One night, Phil must have been sleeping soundly when this happened. He stumbled out of bed, put on his pants, and reached for his shirt. He made his way to the front of the bus, still half asleep, while trying his best to get his shirt on. He seemed to be making a lot of noise, and when I went to investigate I realized he was trying to put my jean skirt over his head! He couldn't for the life of him figure out why it wasn't working. We both had a good laugh before heading on down the road.

Once I was startled by a woman running onto our bus with the query, "Is this the mammogram bus?" I assured her that it was not!

One night we were surrounded by what we believed to be a gang who circled our bus with their cars and trucks, inching closer and closer. It was terrifying. We had a driver then, and he fired up the bus and drove through them. Thankfully they got out of the way. I'm not sure what their intentions were, but I thank God for protecting us.

And there was the time when I didn't want to disturb Phil, who was sleeping and still recovering from surgery. I took matters into my own hands, and may or may not have inadvertently emptied our sewage tank in the wrong place! It was a nightmare, and I'm sure that Olivia and I looked glamorous as we frantically tried to clean up the putrid mess. And just a few hours later when I slid onto the piano bench to play to a full house, no one could have imagined what my hands had been busy with just a few hours before!

I haven't sat behind the wheel of our bus since 2010, and I can't say that I miss it. Those were days when I was just doing what had to be done. Today, we have a full-time bus driver, and I am more grateful for him than I could ever express.

Christmas Tales

A highlight of our year is our Christmas tour. We travel for two weeks, and typically have between ten and twelve one-night Christmas concerts, and while this is labor intensive for us, we so enjoy all the festivities of the season.

My most embarrassing moment on stage happened during a Christmas concert held at the Blue Gate Theatre in Shipshewana, Indiana. This is one of our favorite places, and we've been singing there for many years to packed out auditoriums. Between concerts, we enjoy the amazing cuisine, the Amish bulk-food store where I stock up on homemade noodles and apple butter, the gift shops laden with spicy scented candles and homemade treats, and the sights and smells of the horse drawn carriages with their plain passengers.

We were doing a Christmas concert in a small theatre which seated about four hundred. The place sold out, and there was a fun and festive atmosphere as we walked out onto the stage singing, "It's The Most Wonderful Time Of The Year." The stage was sparkling with trees and lights, and we were all dressed up in our Christmas finery. I was wearing an ivory, floor length dress with long angel-flared sleeves. As the song swelled to a finale, we all began to toss Christmas candy into the audience—a fun moment in the program.

No one had thought to warn us that the lovely decorated balustrade with spindles lining the edge of the stage was not secured. Things went terribly wrong as I walked to the left side and placed my right hand on the railing for leverage while throwing handfuls of candy with my left. The balustrade gave way, and so did I. For one awful moment, I was headed off the stage headfirst, while simultaneously a horrifying mental picture flashed across my mind of *me* upside down in that long, ivory dress. On my way down, I took an awful hit between my eyes from one of the sharp wooden spindles. And, in an all-out effort to avoid going off the stage, I threw myself backwards, wrenching my back, and landing on the stage floor.

I'm not sure how, but I jumped to my feet and finished the song. My head was spinning, my back was killing me, and I instantly knew what it meant to "see stars." Poor Olivia, about ten at the time, stopped singing and stood dumbfounded staring at me...and the blood trickling down my face. I went to the piano bench to play the next number, and somehow made it through. Afterwards, one of the kids handed me a tissue and whispered loudly, "Mom, you're bleeding." I assured the crowd that I was fine, and we finished the concert. I was sore and bruised and sported two lovely black eyes for the rest of the tour. I can laugh about it now, but my face still turns red just thinking what a sight that must have been.

A Hallmark Christmas

In 2017, we were on the last leg of our Christmas tour finishing up concerts in Missouri, Colorado, and Kansas. On an early Friday morning, while still three hours from our next concert venue, I heard an awful noise from the back of the bus. I phoned Phil, who was driving, and told him we'd better stop and check things out. Turns out, there *was* something wrong—something major, and Phil concluded that the bus wasn't drivable.

We were in the middle of nowhere, three hours from our venue, and stranded. There seemed to be no way we would make this date—a sold out concert. In the early days, this would have sent me over the edge with anxiety, but I've learned to sit back, breathe a prayer, and see what God will do.

Phil received a call from Duane Garren, that evening's concert promoter. "Phil, is that you?" he asked. "I just passed you on the interstate." He had hosted another concert in a city east of us the night before and had been on the phone for an extended time that morning, leaving his hotel much later than normal, and just so "happened" to pass our bus sitting beside the road.

Things began to happen in such rapid succession that we could hardly take it all in. The promoter had a friend with a diesel pickup who lived just one exit back. He made a call, and the truck arrived a short time later to take our trailer (with the piano and sound equipment) and the guys on to the venue.

Duane also knew of a bus lease business that just so happened to have one entertainer coach available (this is unheard of - we've typically had to reserve rental buses many weeks in advance). The promoter had also driven right past a bus repair place twelve miles back. The mechanics showed up while he was on the phone with the lease company, while another vehicle appeared to give the rest of us a ride to the shop.

We were a sight! The girls and I scrambled to gather our stage clothes, emptied drawers of toiletries, diapers for babies, shoes, and other items into Wal-Mart or Kroger bags, and traipsed across the highway (the girls in their Christmas pajamas), to the waiting vehicle.

We arrived at the bus repair shop and waited. The people were so kind, and even ordered pizza for us. A while later the rental bus arrived, and off we went in a mad dash to deliver up some CFAM Christmas cheer!

We arrived at the Performing Arts Center less than an hour before concert time. None of us had showered. Duane Garren, in his typical style, had thought of everything! He met us at the bus door, and took us across the street to a brand-new assisted living facility. The director met us at the entrance with an armload of fresh towels, a smile, and a "follow me." As we were ushered down the hall and into brand new rooms with bathrooms, Courtney exclaimed, "Mom, I feel like we're in a Christmas Hallmark movie; at every turn, a stranger is helping us!" I answered, "Let's just hope we all find love in the end!" We quickly showered, got ready, and made it backstage with two minutes to spare.

We had a wonderful evening. I believe the events of the day only added to the Christmas magic in the room. We sang to a sold-out house of 750 merry concertgoers who had no clue what a miracle our presence on stage was that night.

Such is the "glamour" of road life. We collapsed into our beds after midnight, exhausted but grateful for God and strangers who had helped us out along the way.

As for the bus: the mechanic told Phil the next day, "I don't know how the wheels stayed on your bus. The only thing holding them on was loose bolts, and the rotor was broken in half. With the load you were pulling, I don't even want to think about the kind of accident you would have had if the wheels had come off—there must have been someone looking out for you." Phil assured him that indeed there had been—not just "someone," but God in heaven.

Crossing the Border

We have many wonderful friends in Canada and always enjoy our time there. But we've been hung up at the border more times than I care to remember, for a variety of reasons. The following entry from a 2015 journal details just one of those interesting border crossings:

> Crossed the border at 4 a.m. We didn't have to get off the bus and go into customs (thank the Lord). It was strange that around 3 a.m. we were pulled over just before reaching the border. Our bus was searched by the New York State Police. They made everyone show their faces as they were looking for a fugitive who had escaped from a prison nearby. There had been two of them, but one had been shot and killed by police.

It was a frightful thing, waking up and watching the cops pull the bunk curtains back and shine their flashlights into the faces of the occupants. I was just thankful that the fugitive they were looking for *wasn't* on our bus.

And then there was the night when, just as we were preparing to cross over into Canada, a white-faced Michael (Courtney's husband) came to the front and informed Phil that he had completely forgotten to remove his (legal) handgun from the bus. Our bus has been thoroughly searched many times during these border crossings, and we knew that if a weapon was found, we'd be in big trouble. Phil was straightforward, and told the customs officer the truth about the gun. They allowed us to leave it at the border and pick it up on the way back through. We discovered later that Michael had totally forgotten about the *ammunition* he had been given from someone along the way, and stored in the bay. We declared it upon our return, and everything worked out okay.

God's a Good Mechanic

I could fill a book with bus breakdown stories. Phil has often teased that he is a part-time singer and full-time bus mechanic. The bus has become essential equipment for CFAM. It makes our life easier in countless ways, and dealing with the constant issues that arise is just a part of life that we have learned to expect as normal.

I found the following journal entry from 2011, and remember this incident well as the time God "healed" our bus.

> Had a good weekend. Bus started having air pressure issues immediately. Drove two hours thinking it would stop. It continued to get worse and worse. We ended up at a truck stop waiting. The mechanics didn't know what to do for it. The gauges were rapidly vacillating from high to low and beeping. We prayed. Phil stated, "If we don't get this fixed, we won't be making our date in Peterborough, Ontario, tomorrow."
>
> "Let's pray once more," I said. We did. The beeping stopped, the gauges moved into normal range, the bus leveled out, and off we went.
>
> Phil told the mechanic, "We prayed, and it fixed itself." The mechanic replied, "It must have been your prayers because I can't think of a thing I could have done to fix it."
>
> We made it to all our dates last weekend! Thank you, Jesus!

We were finishing up a tour in Canada, and Phil and I had taken a break from the bus. (We do this from time to time.) We were awakened from sleep by a call from the hotel clerk telling us that other customers were complaining about the noise from the bus generator in the parking lot. There was little we could do but move on down the road. I detailed the rest in a journal entry:

> Phil and I got up and went to the bus. Courtney and Olivia were in our bed, so we just moved them to their bunks. We felt bad about that.
>
> Headed to Calgary—what a time we had there. The presence of God was so strong—the people were weeping, laughing, and rejoicing. It was a marvelous night.
>
> Headed for home and made it to South Dakota, about four hours from Sioux Falls. The transmission went out on the bus. This was 1:20 a.m. Monday. After having traveled all day Sunday, the bus was stranded on a two-lane highway in the middle of the road. It would not move. The roads were snow covered, and snow was coming down heavily. It was scary. We turned the engine off and prayed.
>
> We fired up the engine and the bus went into gear for about ten seconds. Just long enough to get it off the road. It wouldn't go back into gear for the rest of the night. We sat there for nine hours until a tow truck came to pull us out. We rode in the back of the bus the entire time we were being towed. It was nerve-wracking feeling the bus shake as semis whizzed past us on the highway.

I will be honest and say that, at times, I've been worn to the bone by the hassles and logistics of travel. But God has shown me time and again that there is a purpose in all of it. Something that is so much bigger than we are. I found the following entry from a journal.

> I'm fighting discouragement. Sometimes I feel like what we're doing out here is not necessary. This morning I walked into Wal-Mart thinking, *How silly of us to be out here, sleeping in Walmart parking lots, dealing with faulty buses; is this even worth it?*
>
> This morning Brandon (our sound guy) read the verse from I Corinthians 15:58. It really encouraged me. It reads:
>
> "Therefore, dear brothers, stand firm. Let nothing move you. Always give yourselves fully to the work of the Lord, because you know that your labor in the Lord is not in vain" (I Corinthians 15:58).

We discovered there were times when the "work of the Lord" had nothing to do with standing on a stage or singing, but just being in the right place at the right time, and being willing to be the hands and feet of Jesus.

While traveling through Nashville, Tennessee, several years ago, we came upon the scene of a gruesome multi-vehicle accident. A tractor trailer had merged onto the highway, hitting another truck and trailer carrying, of all things, a load of cornstarch. The second trailer hit a BMW carrying a family of four. It was chaotic and terrifying—five mangled vehicles littering the cornstarch covered highway and median—and fire!

Someone banged on our bus door asking for our fire extinguisher. Phil grabbed it, and hurried off the bus to lend a hand. We watched from the safety of the bus as Phil and others frantically pulled the mother and a young boy from the BMW SUV. I heard someone yelling, *"Get them out, get them out, it's going to explode!"* We watched, horrified, as the SUV burst into flames, and a father and his precious little girl perished right before our eyes.

I put the children in the back room, as our bus became a triage for a family of five—a mom and four children, who were injured in yet another minivan. They came onto the bus covered in blood and cornstarch, and we laid each of them in a bunk while we waited for help to arrive. Later, I helped carry the kids off the bus and to the waiting ambulance. As the last little girl was being loaded in, I heard someone crying behind me. I turned and found Oliva standing there with her brand new "Build-A-Bear." She wanted to give it to one of the injured children. We quickly placed the bear into the arms of the little girl on the stretcher as she was whisked away to the hospital. I was proud of my sweet girl that day, though we all felt the trauma of that experience for a long, long time.

We have since been in contact and shared the Gospel through music with the widow, her son, and their extended family. God has poured grace into their lives in spite of their unimaginable loss.

Bus Driver Gone Wrong

In the past fifteen years we've experienced just about every 'bus gone wrong' scenario possible, or so we thought. In 2019, we reached a new milestone on our bus-living journey. And this had nothing to do with the bus itself, but a hired bus *driver*.

It was necessary to lease an extra bus for our 2019 Christmas tour. We were carrying more equipment, and had hired extra people to help with the logistics of the tour. We would be an entourage of two buses and two trailers for our two-week schedule of Christmas concerts. The kids playfully dubbed our bus (Black Pearl), which would be carrying Phil, me, Courtney, Michael, and Olivia, the "food bus." I love to feed people, and enjoy stocking everyone's favorite snacks for the road. The lease bus carrying the couples with children, our nanny, and a lighting director, would be the "fun bus."

Our lease bus came with a driver. On the first day, I went onto the *"fun bus"* to make his acquaintance. I introduced myself to a rather gruff and strange acting man. I welcomed him, told him where to find food and snacks, and tried to make him feel at home with us. I thought it somewhat odd that his first question to Lowell, our bus driver had been, "Where's Phil, and when do I get paid?" I felt something was amiss, and reminded him that his passengers were *my children and grandchildren,* and that I would be praying for him as he drove.

I went back to the "food bus" and told Phil and Lowell, "Guys, he's smokin' dope—send him home!" Lowell immediately said, "I'm not sensing that." They rolled their eyes and shook their heads. I was imagining things, they thought; he was fine.

He warmed up to all of us and was friendly for the first four days of our trip. I began to relax, and thought perhaps I was wrong about him. One evening we pulled into the concert venue, and he and Lowell went to the hotel next door to get some rest. We were somewhat surprised when the driver's wife showed up that evening, and they both came to the concert. The kids were excited. We had all been praying for this man, and hoped he and his wife would respond to the message of the Gospel that night. Perhaps this would be another Christmas miracle!

They left at intermission time, and as the night ended and we exited the stage and entered the green room reserved for the artists, Phil was met by two stern-faced police officers. "Are you Phil Collingsworth?" they asked. When he assured them he was, they ordered him to follow them to a private room, where they locked the door and began firing questions at him about our driver.

It seems the CFAM lease bus driver and his wife had been having a little "party" in their hotel room next door during the second half of the concert. Marijuana smoke was wafting through the ventilation system and into the rooms of the other customers throughout this Amish owned hotel. As complaints started pouring into the front desk, the hotel clerk looked up the name for that room, and noted that it was registered to The Collingsworth Family.

Phil assured them that we had only met this guy four days earlier, and that he came as part of our bus lease package.

We never saw the driver again. To think that he would have been driving us through the night in that condition is frightening. And yet, our hearts went out to him, and I pray that he can get to Jesus.

I resisted the strong temptation to say those sweet words to Phil and Lowell, "I told you so!" Lowell did acknowledge that the most difficult part for him was admitting I had been right all along.

This incident left us stranded with no driver, and sold out concerts for the rest of the weekend. Phil called the company and told them that their driver was out of commission! When they told Phil that they had no driver to take his place, Phil insisted that *he* be put on their insurance so that he could drive the "fun bus" until the owner of the company could join us a few days later and finish the tour.

The kids had been posting on social media about the "*food*" and the "*fun*" buses throughout the tour. Even before our bus driver debacle, there had been people showing up to our Christmas concerts with "food bus" vs. "fun bus" signs. People brought food for the "fun bus", and we all enjoyed the friendly rivalry. It wasn't until afterwards that we realized how horribly fitting the term, "fun bus," had been.

The tour ended, and we found that God had redeemed even this unfortunate circumstance. The owner of the company, who ended up driving the rest of the tour for us, said, "Phil, I slipped into two of your concerts on the tour. I don't go to church, but I've realized that I must get my family into church. Can you help me?" Phil was glad to connect him to a pastor we knew from his part of the country.

I'm thankful that God is always working, using every difficulty, redeeming messed up situations, and is always busy bringing about his purposes in the lives of people.

Once we were delayed at the border while leaving Canada, and almost didn't make it to our concert in South Boston, Virginia. Now, I've learned through much experience to rest and trust that God will get us to where we need to be, no matter what impediments we meet along the way, but this time it seemed impossible.

We were finally cleared to cross into the US, and, according to our ETA, we would be arriving at the concert venue a mere forty-five minutes before the scheduled start time. This was a problem. Set-up alone was a four to five-hour ordeal, and included unloading our 7' 6" concert grand piano, a tuning, sound system setup, and sound check. We powered on, and made it on time but had to forgo the piano tuning and other things. At least we were there, in person, standing on stage, and ready to sing. That would have to be enough.

It was the Saturday night before Easter Sunday. Phil and I had spent time in the back of the bus on our way in, carefully putting together our program for the evening. We had prayed together as a team, feeling a bit scattered, and acutely aware of our need for God's help.

I remember our repertoire that night. It included several songs telling of the cross and Christ's sacrifice to redeem sinful men. We sang, "At Calvary," "The Blood of Jesus," and others. God's presence was strong in our weakness that evening.

After the concert, a woman and her seventeen-year-old daughter came to me. This woman was visibly distraught. "I don't even know why I'm here", she said. "Someone gave me two free tickets for my daughter and me. I need to talk to you."

This mother went on to tell me of her sin and the utter hopelessness she felt. "I've lived a horrible life, I've done terrible things, and I recently purchased a handgun with every intention of going into my backyard tonight and ending my life. I just can't do life anymore."

I took her to an empty back row in the auditorium and shared the simple Gospel with her. I told her that there was hope and restoration for her through Christ. That his death and resurrection had made it possible for her to experience freedom from sin and an abundant life. I prayed with her, and she accepted Christ that evening. I'll never forget the sight of her jumping to her feet as if the weight of the world had been lifted from her shoulders.

We were singing that evening, not in a church, but at an American Cancer Society event. The leader was a Christian, and I was able to connect this woman to her for follow-up and care.

As I pondered the events of the day, and how unprepared we had felt at the onset of the evening, I realized that God's Spirit wasn't bound by perfectly tuned pianos, sound checks, or other practices which typically make us feel "ready" for ministry. He wasn't restrained by our weaknesses and limitations that night. He simply needed us to be steadfast, abounding in his work, faithful, prayerful, and relying on him. How freeing this was to me.

11

MEMORABLE PEOPLE, MEMORABLE TIMES

"And sometimes we laugh together,
Sometimes we cry;
Sometimes we share together
Heartaches and sighs.
Sometimes we dream together
Of how it will be
When we all get to heaven,
God's family"[12]

I grew up in a ministry family. My dad served in various capacities as a pastor, evangelist, and Bible college administrator. I didn't understand it when, as a child, I overheard my father say, "Ministry can be a lonely place." He wasn't complaining, just stating a truth that I now, and many who work in ministry, can appreciate.

After giving of ourselves, and expending both spiritual and physical strength, we ministry families can climb into bed at night feeling as if we have a boatload of both admirers and critics, but perhaps only a handful of friends. I am grateful for the people God has strategically placed in

---

12 The Collingsworth Family, *God's Family,* Part of the Family, track #1, Stowtown Records, 2009, DVD & CD

my life over the past twenty years who've "gone beyond the handshake;" Christ-followers who have joined us in the ministry through prayer and support in a hundred different ways; caring people who weren't afraid to insert themselves into my life during tough seasons when I needed them the most.

Phil and I could never find the words to express our gratitude for our... *friends* who have partnered with us on this journey—servant-heart-ed friends who've driven hundreds of miles just to run our product table, generous friends who've brought arm loads of delicious food to the bus, Spirit-led friends who've taken the time to pray for us. We can never re-pay you. You know who you are, and we love you. I could write an entire book about you, but I will only share a few of the ways you have blessed our family.

Very early in the CFAM ministry, we were singing in a certain place when I received the following e-mail from a woman I had only recently met:

> "You've been on my heart and mind for the past several days. I've been praying for you. Last night during the concert, I became to-tally aware of how weary you must be. The music for the camp—four children, a husband, and living out of a van, trailer, and ho-tels. What a life you have…"

I could feel the pathos of the letter at this point and was almost be-ginning to pity myself!

> "I know God is taking care of you, otherwise you'd be in one of those 'mattress covered rooms' somewhere. I am committed to praying for you! I know these next few days will be rough (we were preparing to record). Please know that I am praying for you every day and will do so until I feel God's release."

This precious lady remains a friend today and has *prayed me through* some tough days.

Several years ago, we held a concert at a certain venue in Florida where the promoter was a real challenge. I'm still not sure why he even asked us to come. He was highly critical of the music, and of our Sunday billings policy. And to put it bluntly, his whole demeanor had been angry and rude.

When the bus pulled away from the venue, Phil and I were relieved but also more than a little discouraged. Our spirits sank even further when only a few miles later we experienced a major bus breakdown. Our driver pulled over into a parking lot where we awaited the arrival of a mechanic.

While we waited, I sat on the couch with my Bible open and talked to God. I told him how discouraged I was by the promoter's words and attitude. I worried aloud to the Lord about the current situation with the bus, and was tempted to wonder what we were even doing out here on the road.

At some point, I opened my email and saw a message from a friend of the ministry. The subject line read, "The Holy Spirit asked me to send you an email."

Curious, I opened the letter and read the following passage from Ephesians 3:17b-19:

> "And I pray that you, being rooted and established in love, may have power, together with all the Lord's holy people, to grasp how wide and long and high and deep is the love of Christ, and to know this love that surpasses knowledge—that you may be filled to the measure of all the fullness of God."

Our friend followed up the Scripture quotation with one sentence: *"God told me to tell you that He loves you."*

What a powerful ministry to our hearts that day. The reminder that no matter the criticism, and the difficulties we were currently facing, we were loved by our Heavenly Father. It encouraged us to stay on the path of obedience, and to leave the results to him.

While stopping for fuel one afternoon, we met a young Christian family who happened to be traveling the same way and, like us, had stopped for a brief travel break. Seeing our van and trailer they approached and asked us who we were. We chatted for a while and parted ways. These people have taken the CFAM on as prayer partners, and have prayed for us for two decades. They have sent countless birthday cards, encouraging notes, and monetary gifts to each member of the family. Often their prayers and words have been like honey from heaven during difficult times.

Satan knows where we're most vulnerable, and is brilliant at zeroing in on those vulnerabilities to take us down. I've alluded to the fact that fear and anxiety have threatened to undo me—especially when I'm too busy, facing a deadline, launching into one of Phil's brave visions, or just dealing with change and transition in my personal life.

Not too many years ago, I was in one of these seasons. For several weeks I found myself trembling with fear just before walking onto the stage. It made no sense. I'd been singing and playing piano for decades! Nevertheless, minutes before the beginning of a concert, my heart would begin to pound and my insides quake. It would take three or four songs before my mind would ease and my body relax.

One such night, after singing to a packed-out crowd of twelve hundred, I was approached by the wife of a seminary professor whom I had never met. She introduced herself and went on to say, "Kim, when you walked out on the stage tonight, the Holy Spirit impressed me with the thought, 'You need to pray for that lady.' He prompted me to tell you that, 'You are the daughter of the King, and that *for such a time as this*, God has you in *this place*, sharing *this music* with the world.'" She admonished me to be easy on myself, to rest in the fact that I was God's daughter. I listened intently, gleaning strength and help from her message. I knew this woman was in tune with the Holy Spirit, as her words were exactly what I needed to hear that evening.

During this same season, after suffering through a fearful, sleepless night, I awakened to a message from yet another praying friend:

"I dreamed of you all night long and awakened knowing that God wanted me to share this Scripture with you. 'And now my daughter, don't be afraid. I will do for you all you ask.'" (Ruth 3:11a)

What comfort!

Psalm 107:20 declares, *"He sent forth his Word and healed them."* I'm so thankful for the Word of God, and for the people who have shared it with me in moments when I needed the healing that God's Word delivers.

———————

Many times, God has used my own children to speak truth to me.

It was early 2011, and we were in the middle of a gospel music Mexican cruise. We had ended 2010 rather bombastically when, after months of planning, we had celebrated a large wedding for Brooklyn and Will on the tenth of December. It was a lovely evening with several hundred friends and family. We were thrilled to welcome a new son into the family, but saying "goodbye" to our firstborn had left me weepy and sentimental (my mom readers will identify). Four days after the wedding, Phil had an intricate brain surgery to repair a nerve that had wrapped itself around an artery near his brainstem. He had been suffering for months with severe Trigeminal Neuralgia which had caused his face to draw, moving uncontrollably, and his right eye to twitch continuously and open and close on it's own. His recovery process had been rough.

So here we were on this massive ship, and because of the ages of the kids, Phil and I had to stay in separate staterooms. He was at the other end of the ship on a different floor, while I was in a room with Olivia and Courtney. Phil was feeling lousy, and spent every moment that we weren't singing in his room, mostly sleeping. He was also suffering significant post-surgery depression, which we had not anticipated. Phil typically doesn't get down or despondent. I didn't know what to do with *this* Phil. And although we had just had a big wedding, I was already over my head in planning a June wedding for Courtney and Michael.

To say that I was overwhelmed would be an understatement. I had a sick husband, was planning a wedding, while navigating our regular travel schedule, and was currently singing day after day on a ship out in the ocean in the western Carribean!

Oh, and did I mention that I'm terrified of water? An important detail to this story.

I was awakened one night by a terrible storm. The ship was tossing about on the waves. I sat up and peered through the porthole next to my bed, and saw the angry waves churning and slapping up against the ship as it rolled from side to side. Olivia awakened and sat straight up in bed. "What's happening?" she asked.

"Olivia, there is a terrible storm going on, and I'm scared!" (Not my best mom moment, I know).

Unconcerned, she rubbed her eyes, looked out the small window, yawned sleepily, and said, "Aww *mom, the captain* knows what he's doing." And with that, she fell back onto the bed and into a deep restful sleep.

I sat on the edge of the bed, stricken by the profundity of her words. My life felt very much like this turbulent night on the sea—chaotic, tempestuous, unnerving. And yet, my Captain *did* know what He was doing. With a steadfast love and steady hand He would get us through these rough waters and guide us to safe harbor. God's peace flooded my spirit, and I rested in this truth.

We are blessed with a church family who prays for the CFAM. And then there is my dear friend who, countless times, has dropped a Starbucks card in the mail with a "you're too busy, please take a coffee break" note. These have spawned many "coffee breaks" with my sisters who live in town. Often just what I've needed after a busy weekend on the road.

In Galatians, the Holy Spirit admonishes us to, "Carry each other's burdens, and in this way, you will fulfill the law of Christ." He goes on to say, "Therefore, as we have opportunity, let us do good to all people, especially to those who belong to the family of believers" (Galatians 6:2, 10).

I *cannot* overstate the importance of intercessors and encouragers in the work of the ministry. Those who work in the ministry cannot do it alone. Is God calling *you* to make a difference by committing to pray...*intentionally* and *regularly* for your pastor, or other servants and ministries around the world? When you do, you will, with them, reap the harvest. *Their* fruit is *your* fruit too; their reward, your reward!

To the Corinthians Paul wrote, "...*as you help us by your prayers. Then many will give thanks on our behalf for the gracious favor granted us in answer to the prayers of many*" (2 Corinthians 1:11).

Phil and I are blessed with wonderful families. And although the years have taken us to different places in life, there is always something wonderful about coming back together.

The Keaton family began a tradition many years ago of holding a biennial family reunion. With my parents and all nine of us children and our ever-growing families, this is no small endeavor. The sheer volume of people results in a good amount of mayhem and confusion, but any discomforts pale in comparison to the love and laughter and camaraderie we find from each other's company.

In November of 2005, the CFAM was gaining some momentum. We had kept our heads down, working, praying in the funds to grow the ministry, and trusting God for spiritual blessing on our music. Looking back, I see that we had become perhaps a little too self-focused.

We were singing in Lakeland, Florida, that week for a four-day conference, but I had been on the phone with several of my siblings. We were busy planning for our Keaton Family Reunion which was to take place in June.

I was awakened early one morning with a strong impression that Phil and I were to fund bringing my sister Becky, her husband, Tim, and their five children "home" for this reunion. They were serving as missionaries in the Philippines, and had no plans of coming home that year. This was not the first reunion they had missed due to living overseas, but this one was especially hard, as none of us had met our newest niece, Samantha, who had been born in Manila the previous August.

I sat up on the side of the bed and thought, *Lord, is this you?* There is no way we could fund something this big. I didn't know how much it would cost to fly a family of seven from Southeast Asia, but I knew it would be more money than I could lay my hands on. I walked to the front of the bus and told Phil what I was thinking. He immediately said, "Kim, we need to do this!"

As I started thinking about the amount of money we would need to pull this off, the Lord reminded me of a check that I had tucked away in my wallet.

In those days, Phil would sometimes go to a car auction, purchase cars, and sell them. We had purchased a car a few months back, drove it for a short time, and then sold it on Ebay. We actually enjoyed this kind of thing, and Phil would often give me the extra money for household items—clothes for the children, etc. We had earned $2,000 on this particular car, and I had stashed it away.

I felt the Lord say, "Kim, what about the $2,000?" I pulled it out and looked at it, thinking, *This is all the extra money we have!* We didn't even have a savings account in those days. Every penny we earned was going straight back into the ministry.

Phil called the kids to the sitting area of the bus and explained what we were planning. He told them that mom was giving her two thousand dollars, and that we would pray in the rest. He got a big jar and put it on the counter, stating that this was our "reunion money jar," and that every extra dime that came in would go into the jar. The kids were ecstatic! The thought of their cousins coming home sent them jumping up and down with excitement. We also decided that we would keep it a secret. We didn't know how we'd do it, but we were going to surprise the entire

Keaton family by having Tim and Becky, along with their five children, knock on the front door on the first night of reunion. We emphasized the importance of keeping this quiet. I'm only thankful that social media hadn't been discovered, as it would have been impossible, I'm sure.

I had to call Becky next, as she had no idea of the plans we were already making. I asked her if it would be possible for them to get away for a few weeks, if the expenses were taken care of. She was excited at the prospect, and after talking to Tim, who made some ministry arrangements, they let us know it was a go.

Over the next few weeks answers to prayer tumbled over one another, as little by little the reunion jar filled up. There was a woman who bought $120 in products and wrote a check for $300—$180 extra. In the jar it went! Phil came on the bus one evening calling out to the children, "Hey kids, look what someone handed me tonight!" as he pulled a $500 check out of his pocket and dropped it into the jar.

Then, late one night after a concert as we were loading up, a lone truck pulled into the lot and parked right in front of the bus. A man exited the truck, and came to the bus. "I don't know why but I feel like I'm supposed to give you this," he began, as he pulled a piece of paper out of his pocket. He paused a moment, expressing his appreciation for a song we had sung the night before titled, "Leave a Legacy." He was grappling with the loss of his mother, and wanted to do something in honor of her. With that he handed Phil a check for $1,000. We thanked him *profusely*, and added it to the growing amount in the jar.

We were astounded as night after night God added to the amount we needed to make this dream a reality.

We were almost to our goal when we were offered two extra concerts which went beyond our "nine dates a month" policy. We talked it over as a family, and agreed that we would take these concerts, and trust God to bring in the rest of the needed funds. And when the honorariums for those two concerts were...*to the penny* what we needed to finish filling our jar, we really weren't surprised. We were learning more about the character of God. When he asks us to do something, he always provides the ways and means.

By May, we had saved enough money to buy tickets, purchase a van for the duration of Tim and Becky's eleven week stay (we sold the van afterwards), update the children's wardrobes, and cover all other expenses incurred while they were in the USA. And although we didn't know it at the time, it had been a very difficult season of ministry for my sister and her husband. God was providing what *he knew* they needed, without them even asking. And God allowed us to be in on the fun! It was awesome!

We took the bus to the airport to pick them up, and hid them at our home for a couple of days while they recovered from jet lag. The house was full of chaotic happiness, as the cousins made up for lost time. And we all loved on sweet, ten-month-old Samantha.

I could hardly believe we had pulled this off, and when we surprised the whole clan—all 60-plus of them—when Tim and Becky and the kiddos walked into the room, there was a beautiful cacophony of screaming, tears, laughter, and a lot of, "*How in the world* did you *do* this!?"

I love traveling, but I love being home as well. I am a hopeless idealist when it comes to the nostalgia of family, holidays, and old-fashioned tradition. God has blessed us with a home where I have room to host our large family and extended family for Thanksgiving each year. We serve up endless amounts of delicious food, and I'm known to my nieces and nephews for filling every candy dish in the house with their favorites. We sing and worship, play games, and talk for hours. I love it all!

For some years we went caroling on Christmas Eve. The CFAM would head out with other family members in town, or those visiting. We'd sing to shut-ins, or sometimes surprise good friends with a little festive music. For several years, we caroled each year at local hospitals. It warmed our hearts to see the joy it brought to patients and their families who were suffering and confined.

One year we decided to attend a Christmas Eve service with my sisters and their families. Our home church wasn't hosting one, so we made plans to drop in at a small country church near our home. At 11 p.m. we stepped into the tiny foyer where we—all twenty-one of us—were handed white candles and invited to take a seat. We nearly filled the small chapel, and when I counted all the attendees, we totaled thirty-one; twenty-one of us, and ten of them. When the leader directed the small audience to sing the first carol, "Joy to the World," our voices filled up the room. We spent an hour reading Scripture and singing our way through the Christmas story.

As the pastor closed the service, his eyes filled with tears and he thanked us for coming. "I prayed that we would have six attendees tonight," he stated. "You all have made my Christmas!" He and the kind people of that little church had made ours! It was an unforgettable night; one of quiet simplicity and reflection.

While driving past this church a few days later, I was startled to see their church sign which read, "Many thanks to The Collingsworths for Christmas Joy—Songs."

I would surmise that I've sat on some type of stage ministering through music to a variety of audiences several thousand times in my life. I could share dozens of unforgettable moments, but will choose only a few that are burned into my memory.

While singing at Gaither Family Fest in Gatlinburg, Tennessee sometime in 2007 or 2008, we experienced every musician's worst nightmare. We were to perform a four number set that night, with not only our colleagues seated around us, but an enthusiastic audience of seven thousand. Our track to an upbeat song we had recently recorded started up and we began to sing,

> I shall not be moved,
> I shall not be moved,
> I'm anchored to the rock,
> Standing on the truth,
> And I shall not be moved.[13]

This song includes several verses, key changes, and intricate five-part harmonies. We were right in the middle of the arrangement when the equipment malfunctioned and the track went silent.

The kids all looked at me wide-eyed as I quickly gave them the signal to keep singing. We continued barreling through the song while huddled in a semi-circle and feeling like we were in the middle of that nightmare—you know the one where you are on the platform at church...only partially clothed...or not!? I'm not sure how but we made it through every part and key change of that song. I discovered later that some of our friends were betting on whether or not we'd pull it off.

We lost *every sound track* that night and when the track to my final number failed, a piano solo, How Great Thou Art, I quickly transitioned to an old favorite—one my mom used to play—When They Ring Those Golden Bells. I made the decision based on two factors: the "seasoned" age of the audience—they would know this song—and I knew I wouldn't need a track. We discovered later that a faulty headphone jack on Phil's laptop had been the culprit.

I found a journal detailing what happened one evening last year when we all were suffering with sickness which had left our voices hoarse and unreliable:

> In Bremen, Georgia, at Miltown Music Hall, all five of the six voices were down all at once. This has never happened in our history of singing. It was scary!
> On Friday night in Hattiesburg, Mississippi, we literally broke down on "This is My Father's World" (an a cappella arrangement). We made it through, but it sounded like an off-key train wreck. Hilarious and scary all at once.

---

13 The Collingsworth Family, *I Shall Not Be Moved*, track #1, The Answer, Crossroads Records, 2011, CD

I will never forget Phillip's large round eyes as he pulled his "ears" (audio earpiece) out in the middle of what should have been a six-part harmonious sensation and stared at me with a look that shouted, "*What is happening!?*" It was definitely sensational—but for all the wrong reasons.

We have sung at some unique venues—places I didn't really envision our music taking us. I won't forget the first time we were asked to sing at a county fair...on a Sunday night. I was hesitant to accept the date. For some reason it seemed almost sacrilegious, going to a county fair on a Sunday for *any* reason. I grew up not going to county fairs at all, as my mother didn't care for the atmosphere. I argued with Phil that we should be in church on Sunday evening and not at a fairground. Phil was insistent that we take the date—that we "Sing Jesus at the county fair!" So I did what I've done many times in my earlier years; I called my dad.

When I explained the situation and asked dad, "What do you think we should do?" He didn't hesitate. "Well, if they'd ask me to come and *preach* at a county fair, I'd do it." He went on, "Jesus would go there, Kimberly; he'd go wherever there were people who needed him."

On the night of the event as I watched from our bus window, the "stage," a large flatbed trailer, was pulled into the middle of a horse corral. I turned to the girls and said, "This will be a casual dress tonight, you can even wear your flip flops." The guys unloaded "Lucille," our 7'6" Yamaha concert grand piano onto that trailer, and by the time the concert started, nearly a thousand people were standing or sitting in the bleachers and around the perimeter. The evening was fantastic! God showed up, although we did have to compete with the noise of a tractor pull happening nearby.

I talked to many people after the county fair concert who were touched by the music and the message it delivered. One lady wistfully expressed the need she felt to get her children back into church. It occurred to me that while we *hadn't* been in a church building that night, we *had* brought Christ to the county fair. I believe it made him smile.

Another time we held a benefit concert for a children's home in Tallahassee, Florida; one which houses girls ages thirteen to eighteen. We enjoyed interacting with these precious girls, touring their home, and listening as they shared some of their heartbreaking stories with us.

At the end of the concert, the girls joined us on stage and sang, "That's the Place I'm Longing to Go." It touched me deeply, hearing them sing these lyrics:

> Where the orphan has a home,
> Where nobody is alone,
> That's the place I'm longing to go.[14]

Phil was like a kid when we were called to sing for a share-a-thon for radio station, WEEC, in Dayton, Ohio. This was the station Phil had spent hours listening to as a young boy, and for me to watch as Phil went on the air with *the* Uncle Charlie—the man who had captivated Phil and countless other kids with his stories and Bible lessons—was epic. We developed a warm friendship with Uncle Charlie and his wife Betty, which lasted until his death several years ago.

I've discovered that God will show up anywhere in any place where His name is lifted up...even if *He* isn't on the program.

While setting up for a concert one evening, a certain promoter slid onto the piano bench while Phil was adjusting some equipment, and said, "Hey Phil, just so you know, we're not here to have church, just a singing."

When Phil gave me the message, I must admit I was appalled. I thought, *Well, I guess if God shows up tonight, we'll ask Him to leave.* I'm not trying to be unkind or self-righteous. Truth is, I don't know how to operate in the realm of "just singing." We sing the Gospel! It's what we

---

14 The Collingsworth Family, *That's the Place I'm Longing to Go*, track #11, Part of the Family, Stowtown Records, 2009, CD

do! We give praise to God through music, and I don't want to do it without Him being present.

That night God's presence was palpable as the people praised and worshipped. I lost my timidity as I grabbed the mic and told the crowd, "I know we're not supposed to have church tonight, but if Jesus shows up, we're having church!"

I think the promoter forgave me, and he was kind. I figured he didn't have to ask us back if we weren't the kind of group he was looking for. To our surprise, he did extend another invitation.

We sang one night at First Baptist Church in Indian Trail, North Carolina to a crowd of 2,000. There was a 180-voice-choir backing us up, and God's presence was especially near.

I don't know what was going on in the lives of the audience that evening, but as the kids sang, "I Can Trust Jesus," a sweet and powerful spirit of praise filled the room. I will never forget what happened as the kid's sang those beautiful words,

> He is my strong tower,
> The strength in my weakest hour,
> I can trust Jesus, he takes care of me.[15]

I can only describe it as a wave of the presence of God that moved from one side of the building to the other. People stood to their feet weeping with their hands in the air.

We had sung to thousands of audiences, but this night left an indelible impression on us all. And the kids talked for days about the presence of God they'd witnessed first-hand that evening.

I journaled about it and ended my entry with:

> Thank you, Jesus—please let us see more of you.

---

15 The Collingsworth Family, *I Can Trust Jesus*, track # 7, We Still Believe, Crossroads Records, 2007, CD

The year 2019 brought two most unexpected opportunities.

In April, we traveled to Washington, DC, to sing for the National Day of Prayer kick-off banquet. It was an amazing experience. A highlight of the evening was meeting Dr. and Mrs. James Dobson. I expressed my appreciation for the ways in which Dr. Dobson's ministry had helped me raise my children. We met former congressman, Bob McEwen, and his lovely wife, Liz. They took us on a late-night tour of the Capitol Building. It was mesmerizing, and I wrote in my journal:

> ...Very much a pinch myself kind of experience.

Then, through an amazing chain of unexpected events, we were invited to perform Christmas music at the White House on December 20, 2019. It was surreal, sitting on the bus and looking out the window as we rolled through those formidable gates and up the long driveway to America's most famous residence. We sang for more than two hours in the East Room, under the watchful eye of George Washington, whose original portrait (the one that Dolly Madison rescued as she fled the White House as it burned during the War of 1812) hung on the wall behind us. Hundreds of federal workers and their families filed through the room, stopping to listen as they admired First Lady Melania Trump's stunning and unparalleled décor. We toured the White House later that day, and I thought it unbelievable that this had been our final performance, not only of 2019, but of twenty years of the CFAM ministry. And what a way to celebrate!

As a little girl, I couldn't have imagined that God would allow me so many wonderful opportunities to share *His* gift with the world. I am beyond grateful for each one of them.

12

JOY IN A CANCELED WORLD

God's plans have not been canceled;
He's still in control,
And everything that matters still remains.
—Kim Collingsworth

On January 10, 2020, I headed into a Hobby Lobby store with my daughter Olivia, where I planned to scoop up some amazing after-Christmas sales. As we browsed the sparse leftovers of the season, a wooden sign caught my eye. On it, the word JOY was emblazoned in festive red. I paused, pointed to it, and said, "Olivia, see that sign? That's my word for 2020."

Joy had been on my mind for days. During my Bible reading, God had been impressing this word upon my heart. I had sensed him say to me, "Kim, *joy* is your word for 2020. I want you to pursue joy."

My daily Scripture reading had taken me to many passages which addressed this matter of joy. Among many, I read,

> "You make known to me the path of life; you will fill me with *joy* in your presence, with eternal pleasures at your right hand" (Psalm 16:11).

In the book of John, after expressing his love for his children, Jesus went on to say,

"These things I have spoken to you, that My *joy* may remain in you, and that your *joy* may be full" (John 15:11 NKJV).

Nehemiah told the weeping people of his day,

"This day is holy to our Lord. Do not grieve, for the *joy* of the Lord is your strength" (Nehemiah 8:10b).

This emphasis on joy was good for me. I was enjoying my study immensely, and it seemed at every turn, this word was popping up, reminding me of its importance. I even wrote about it in a journal entry, not knowing how this study would come to bear in my life in the very near future.

> March 12, 2020
>
> Back on the bus singing three dates this weekend. The Coronavirus is really threatening our dates right now—trusting Jesus about this. We had a wonderful Bible study last night. It was exactly what we needed. The study was on "Joy," the very topic I've been studying myself. Thank you, Lord. Joy is in direct relationship and proportion to our time spent in prayer and focus on the promises of God. I believe this so much!

Reading my journal reference to the Coronavirus *now*, months later, sounds a bit calloused and superficial. But did any of us comprehend on March 12, 2020, just how the "pandemic" would alter life as we knew it? Did we grasp the enormity of suffering that would ensue? Not only from the virus, but from the loss of jobs, livelihoods, and even loved ones? Could we have known the chaos into which our nation and the world would descend as a result of political and social upheaval? Of course not.

When we turned the bus toward home on Saturday evening, and settled in for a late-night arrival the following day, the unthinkable began to happen. One by one, our upcoming concert dates began to evaporate, as uncertainty and fear gave way to caution and shutdowns in this strange new pandemic world. The bus pulled onto Brannon Road sometime after 10 p.m. on Sunday evening, and the team all scattered to their own homes. Phil and I ended up in the kitchen, where we sat until 5:30 a.m. We tried to wrap our minds around the phenomena taking place, and attempted to make a game plan. And while we sat processing, the cancellations just kept coming.

> March 21
>
> It's unreal how one week can literally change the way life operates. We sang last week in Peoria, Illinois; Branson, Missouri; and Keene, Texas, not having a remote comprehension that we would not be singing again for at least eight or nine weeks.

Eight or nine weeks!? I'm smiling as I read those words. The truth is, to date, more than two-thirds of The Collingsworth Family concerts have been canceled in 2020. But I'm not telling you anything you, my reader, do not understand. No doubt your life and family have also been impacted by the year 2020, by the events we've all experienced—and *survived* together.

In the ensuing days, it dawned on me that I would have to do battle for the *joy* about which I had been studying and journaling. My melancholy personality lends itself to anxiety and despair when things become uncertain. I realized that anxiety and joy are mutually exclusive. They cannot reside in the same heart at the same time.

One morning, I sat in my favorite chair drinking coffee with an open Bible on my lap. My reading took me to Philippians 4:4-6 where I read:

> "Rejoice in the Lord always. I will say it again: Rejoice! Let your gentleness be evident to all. The Lord is near. Do not be anxious about anything, but in everything by prayer and petition, with thanksgiving, present your requests to God. And the peace of God, which transcends all understanding, will guard your hearts and your minds in Christ Jesus."

My good friend Babbie Mason once said, "If you want to hear God's voice, open up your Bible." I wrote those words down and have never forgotten them.

That morning, as I sat out in *"The Haven,"* a place I'll share more about in a moment, meditating on the living Word of God, I heard his voice. It was as if he came and sat beside me and helped me discern my own personal path to joy—joy I could know even in the midst of job loss, pandemic, and total uncertainty.

> "Kim, I want you to do three things. I want you to:
> Rejoice in me always
> Be gentle to everyone
> Don't be anxious about *anything,* but give thanks for *everything.*"

The mandate was clear. I was to praise the Lord every day, no matter what happened. I was to rejoice in his goodness, his faithfulness, his mercy, his kindness. I was to show great delight in who he is—rather than fretting over what was going on in the world around me.

I chuckled to myself as I mulled over God's directive to me on this matter of gentleness. He knows me so well. To be quarantined for weeks on end—even with those we love most—requires an extra dose of gentleness. God was reminding me not to allow the stress of these days to spill over into frustration, anger, or impatience. I was to put on the gentleness of Christ.

Finally, I was to renounce the enemy of anxiety. God is very explicit with this command: "Don't be anxious about *anything"—anything* happens to be, according to the dictionary, *any event, act, object, or situation.* Yep, I think that covers...well, *anything!* But I was to be thankful for *everything,* a pronoun that means *to encompass all.*

You and I aren't the first to find ourselves in a situation in which thankfulness seems impossible.

In her book, *The Hiding Place,* Corrie Ten Boom tells how she and her sister Betsy were thrown into a European concentration camp during WWII as punishment for hiding Jews in their home. Corrie prayed for ways to share her faith even while being held in a most deplorable bunker, crawling with bedbugs.

One day while meditating on the verse I quoted from Philippians 4, Betsy pointed out to Corrie that perhaps they should give thanks for the bedbugs. "After all," she stated, "the verse says, 'In *everything* give thanks.'" But as Corrie sat scratching the sores on her body she said aloud, "I cannot thank God for this!"

Reluctantly, at the prompting of her sister, Corrie thanked God... *"even for the bedbugs,"* and tried to make the best of their situation. Soon after, God opened the door for her to evangelize many women who were housed in that miserable place. They held Bible studies freely as the guards rarely came inside.

One afternoon, when a couple guards came into the bunker to retrieve a dead body, Corrie overheard them discussing why they never entered this bunker. It was simple—they couldn't abide the bedbugs!

For a *glorious moment*, Corrie glimpsed the extraordinary way God had used the cause of her suffering—thousands of blood-sucking bed bugs—to bring the hope of the Gospel to many women! Wow!

Because we live in a fallen world, we will suffer. The beautiful truth is, however, that there is nothing—not a pandemic, financial loss, sickness, death, broken relationship, or...you fill in the blank...that can thwart the redemptive purposes of God in the lives of his children. He will always have the last word in our suffering, if we choose to trust him—even *thank* him—right in the middle of our problem.

God assured me that morning, if I would rejoice, be gentle, turn away from worry, and give thanks for everything—even in this interruption, with all the uncertainty it represented—he would in return:

- Guard my heart. He would put a bulletproof vest over my most vital organ and protect my most vulnerable place—the seat of my affections from which everything else flows.
- Guard my mind. As I continued exploring what God's Word has to say about the mind, it became clear that I had the tools and a responsibility to protect my mind from becoming the devil's playground.

Through the Word of God, the Holy Spirit spoke peace to my heart. I sensed him say, "I will get you and your family through this difficult time. Just follow me and obey my Word."

Joshua 1:8 admonishes to, "Keep this Book of the Law always on your lips; meditate on it day and night so that you may be careful to do everything written in it. Then you will be prosperous and successful."

So often, I have been guilty of talking too much about my problems—those words which stir up emotions, upset me, and cause me to put excessive focus on my circumstances. I understand that we must face the reality of adverse situations, but doing so without keeping the Word and the promises of God on our lips will lead us to give far too much credence to our circumstances. Sometimes we need to work at keeping our *minds* and our *mouths* off of the problem.

I began to see that focusing on the Word of God, and the truth found in it, was how I would experience the transcendent peace of God—right now, in the middle of our new upside down world.

With a new awareness of God's sovereignty in everything, Phil and I took a deep breath and called a team meeting in those first few weeks of lockdown.

We were not alone on this sea of vulnerability. Many of our friends were also attempting to navigate the rough water of uncertainty and trying, as we were, to come up with creative solutions.

We had a wonderful time of prayer together, and began discussing options for the CFAM. Could we continue to sing? From home? Should we charge a fee for online viewing? Would people even pay to watch? *God, we need to work. What do you want us to do?*

Earlier in the week, I had played a piano request livestream which went for nearly an hour and a half. I did this on a whim, just feeling the need to reach out and encourage others who were feeling, perhaps, the weight of our world situation just as I was. I honestly didn't know for sure if people would get on and watch. It was astounding to me that by the end of the evening we had nearly ten thousand viewers (devices) worshipping online with me.

As we sat in The Haven and talked as a family regarding the CFAM ministry going forward, I felt a little nudge from the Holy Spirit.

I spoke up and began with a premise, "Guys, I'm going to just throw something out—God won't let us down—he has a good track record."

"What if," I continued, "we do the online concert, charge a fee, and.... give the proceeds away! Let's find a ministry which desperately needs assistance during this pandemic, and let's give the money away."

After a bit more dialogue, we scrapped the fee altogether, deciding to open it up free of charge to anyone. We were thinking especially of those stranded at home, many alone and separated from family and friends.

It was unanimous. We all felt strongly that this was right. The concert would be free, but we would provide a "donate" button, and every penny would go to assist the faith-based organization/charity that we had yet to choose.

Phil got busy exploring different opportunities. We have enjoyed a long-standing relationship with the people at the Billy Graham Training Center, otherwise known as The Cove. And when Phil learned that Samaritan's Purse, an organization headed up by Franklin Graham, was assembling a field hospital for Covid-patients in a disease-flooded area in New York City, it was unanimous. This would be our project.

As we prepared for the evening, we spent $1,000 for equipment rental. Will and Michael (our sons-in-law) would do the filming, and spent time practicing. Olivia suggested, instead of pre-recording, as we had planned, it should be a livestream. We spent a few evenings around the piano singing hymns and gospel songs, and then carefully chose the ones we would include on the livestream. Interestingly enough, of the fourteen songs we chose, nine of them we had never sung before as a family. They just seemed to fit the situation and the times we were in. It felt right.

I felt God's joy and peace begin to take residence in my heart, even as the world around us descended into chaos. One day, I sat at the piano reflecting on how all our lives as we had known them—our jobs, plans, churches, means of worship, and so much more—had been canceled. There was nothing that hadn't been affected by this new reality in which we all found ourselves. And yet, it occurred to me, that for the believer, all that mattered still remained.

The words came, and I sang them aloud as I played,

> When life is put on hold,
> All our plans have canceled;
> Things have changed,
> Nothing feels the same.
> Disappointments, fear and doubt
> Go hand in hand,
> And waves of worry threaten me,
> Everywhere uncertainty.
>
> But in the midst of chaos,
> In the midst of fear,
> There is something to remember;
> Yes, there is something we all need to hear:
>
> Joy is not canceled,
> Peace still remains;
> God's goodness, kindness,
> His grace isn't running low,
> And he has not changed.
> His power is still abundant,
> His mercies are still new;
> God's plans have not been canceled;
> He's still in control,
>
> And everything that matters still remains.[16]

16 The Collingsworth Family, *Joy is not Canceled*, track #12, Worship from Home, Stowtown Records, 2020, DVD & CD

I finished the song, and though I felt it was still rough, and didn't plan to include it on the livestream, the kids talked me into doing so.

We really had no idea how much money would come in for the hospital, but just before the cameras started rolling, Phil announced, "Guys, I'm believing God for $10,000." The girls piped up with, "Nope, we think it will be $25,000." I looked at the whole lot of them and exclaimed, "Well, I'm asking for $50,000!" We were excited at the prospect of joining with so many of our friends to make a difference for those suffering in New York City. Looking back, I think God was smiling at our attempt to think "big."

March 29, 2020, was a wonderful, impromptu evening of worship. God's presence was so real in The Haven. And as we sang, people continued to log on—25,000 (devices) joined us to listen, to worship...and to give. The numbers kept rising, and when the night was over the stats showed that 200,000 people had viewed the concert, and every penny of the $234,000 donated was given to Samaritan's Purse! Yes! You read that right! God's people had stepped up and overwhelmed us by their generosity. The $1,000 we had invested in the equipment was also taken care of unexpectedly. The following week a check arrived in the mail from a dear friend of our ministry with instructions to "put it toward any expenses incurred for the livestream." We were astounded! Grateful! And we continue to give all the glory to God who made it happen.

The following morning, I sat out in The Haven lingering long over my coffee while I gazed around the room noting the general disarray. Various pieces of equipment were here and there, along with copies of our song list. Furniture which had been shoved out of the way now sat at awkward angles. I took in all the remnants of the previous evening's livestream, while my mind darted back...*way* back, to a dream God had given me several years earlier—a dream which led to the inception of this place we now call The Haven. And it's a story worth telling.

It was the beginning of 2015, and I was feeling restless in my spirit. I was plenty busy as the ministry was humming. We were enjoying all the opportunities coming our way. But I felt there was something I was to do…something I needed to ask and receive from the Lord. But I didn't have a clue what it could possibly be. I journaled my thoughts:

January 6, 2015

God, I need a less scattered focus. I seem to be running here and there, really getting nothing of significance done. Realign my focus. I want to have a God honoring dream to do something eternally impacting for you. Focus me. What is that audacious God-sized dream? Show me, Lord!

What I am going to say here sounds perhaps a little crazy. What happened in the following months doesn't in any way align with my personality. I have told you numerous times in this book that Phil is the dreamer, the visionary, the man always gazing beyond the horizon. I'm Phil's cautious, reticent, bean-counting, number-crunching counterpart. This is the truth!

All through the spring and summer of 2015, I kept having the reoccurring thought that we needed to build a room onto our home. A large room, upper and lower.

I envisioned a lower room studio—a studio like the one I had dreamed of as a child. My very own studio. No more trips to far off places to record our music. A place where I could have my coffee in my own chair before heading down to record our music. A place where we could help other artists record their music, too.

The upper room would serve as a venue for future live videos, Bible studies, large family gatherings, and a warm and comfortable place where Christian community and fellowship would take place.

I kept this to myself, not even telling Phil until the weekend of our anniversary in September. We were enjoying a quiet morning together, just sitting in the living room, when I said, "Phil, I've been thinking...."

I went on to share what I'd been mulling over in my mind for so many months.

After I picked Phil up off the floor!...he, of course, hopped on board immediately. He jumped out of his chair and went to get a tape measure to see just how big this room would be. It didn't necessarily reassure me, as Phil is the guy who, if offered the suggestion of building a replica of the Empire State Building in the woods behind our house, would probably say, "We can try it!" Funny thing is, he'd probably get it done, too! And for me to be the one suggesting such a thing, well, it was thrilling for Phil, and he wasn't going to miss out on this—no way, no how!

It took time, of course, to secure builders and make our plans to proceed. We were set to break ground in May of 2018, but as the date inched closer, I went into "typical Kim mode" and began to second-guess myself.

I remember sitting in my office early one morning. I sipped my coffee and gazed out the window at the emerald trees that lined the edge of our woods, while worrisome scenarios played havoc with my mind.

What have I done? What if this is a mistake? What if we can't pay for this room? And then, in desperation, I said aloud, "Lord, please reveal the foolishness of this to Phil, and if this is not your will, use him to shut this down." Moments later, Phil walked into the office and said, "Kim, I feel such confirmation about this new room." He had my attention; I had just been praying that God would speak to him. He continued on, "Just this morning I felt the Lord impress upon me that we should proceed with this new room unless, for some reason, he stops us."

I am a bit like Gideon, and in just a few days was overwhelmed again by this daunting commitment we were taking on. Once again, I prayed, "Lord, if this is not your will, please let our builders cancel." They were coming in May to break ground, and we were still in March. That afternoon, I received a call from Phil who was out of town. "Kim," he said, "the builders called today. They're way ahead of schedule and want to move our groundbreaking to April." How much more confirmation did I need?

On the day they poured the footers, I waited until the builders were gone before walking outside. I stood there in the fresh dirt, full of fear at the prospect of what we were taking on, and *yet* I heard the words come out of my mouth, "Phil, I think it's too small." He looked at me, dumbfounded, and said, "Kim, how big do you want this room to be?" I had no answer for him, but my instinct told me this room was too small. The God-sized dream for this room did not match up with where these footers were poured. We did some configurations on our own, and our builder graciously agreed to extend the room to make it an even 1,400 square feet.

A few days after the footers were poured, the basement walls started going up. I stood at the window and watched with the all too familiar stomach twisting uncertainty. "God, why am I so afraid?" I heard him say to me, "Kim, this is your Noah's Ark. You don't know exactly how I'm going to use this room, but you're going to have to trust me."

On March 29th, when the livestream was finished and the kids had gone home, I walked back out into The Haven and stood gazing out the window into the darkness. My heart was full and I leaned into the moment reveling in God's goodness. I knew that something of significance had taken place that evening. And more importantly, I knew that it was only the tip of the iceberg of God's purpose for this room.

I thought of the remaining balance owed to finish paying for The Haven, and felt strongly that I was to ask God to help us pay for it—while we were off work—every penny of it. In the stillness I bowed my head and breathed my simple request.

I must admit that it took time to settle in, exhale, and accept the fact that we weren't going anywhere to sing for the foreseeable future. Every single day there were more dates being canceled. I thought back to the days when I had longed for such a rest as was forced upon us now. I looked back, and found my journal entry from January, where I had written:

> God help us not to be so scattered in the way we live. We're so busy! Jesus, give us restraint.

Slowly I began to allow myself to lean into the new normal. As I stayed focused on the Word of God and his promises, I began to relax, and felt the worry and tension dissipate. I would write the following in April:

> It's 2:29 p.m. and as of this writing I'm completely relaxed. Still in my pajamas. Crazy! Totally trusting Jesus to provide our every need. So glad I know the Lord.

The question, "How long can we live without working?" didn't necessarily go away. Phil and I took turns holding the banner of "what if." On the days he was up, I'd hang on to it, and when I felt hopeful, Phil would take his turn at worrying about the future of the CFAM.

There was a day when the steady stream of cancellations was getting the best of Phil. He left the room to go and shower. I was still in my chair reading God's Word, and asking the Lord to speak his truth to me, when suddenly the words from I Corinthians 15:58 leaped off the page and illuminated my mind.

> "Therefore, my dear brothers and sisters, stand firm. Let nothing move you. Always give yourselves fully to the work of the Lord, because you know that your labor in the Lord is not in vain."

I wrote the words on a 3x5 card and took them to our bedroom. I heard the shower running, so I opened the shower door, and held the card up. "Phil, this is our word from God for today!" I exclaimed.

I felt so strongly that no matter what, we were to keep working for the Lord. Right here, right now, in our home, from our home, in whatever ways he provided, and through any door he chose to open. And I somehow knew that just as he promised, it would not be in vain.

Something beautiful began to happen with The Haven during those long weeks at home. We were given opportunities to use this room to provide music to churches all over the USA and around the world. As livestream became the mode of ministry for churches and organizations everywhere, I began to see the sovereignty of God in providing such a place where we could continue sharing his gift of music, even in the midst of a pandemic.

In addition to 2 piano livestreams, we have also recorded:

1. The *Worship from Home* fundraiser for Samaritan's Purse
2. Easter worship for the Brooklyn Tabernacle
3. Special worship for First Baptist Columbia, South Carolina
4. We provided interactive worship, and the venue for the special communion service of the Bible Methodist Connection of Churches, which was aired on Easter Sunday to their churches around the world.
5. A "get-out-the-vote" evening, with special speaker, Congressman Bob McEwen
6. And we are currently preparing to film Christmas worship to be played for The Brooklyn Tabernacle, and also the North Rome Church of God, in Rome, Georgia.

When God gave me the dream to build The Haven in 2015, my plans for the room could not have encompassed all that God knew was coming in 2020, and the ways in which he would use it for our good and his glory. God was right—it is our "Noah's Ark." And he is using it in many ways through the ministry opportunities it has afforded, to save our family. Also, you'll be thrilled to know as a side note, he has also answered my prayer. The room—his room— is *completely* paid for, and its story has not yet been fully told. What a wonderful God we serve.

Perhaps you are reading this today and are weighed down by the difficulties you are facing. Perhaps 2020 has brought the unthinkable in your life. Maybe you feel alone in your suffering. While I do not know what your burden is today, nor what the future holds for any of us, there is one thing of which I am certain. I *do* know that the Lord God is not finished with the CFAM, and he is not finished with *you*. I know that the Word of God is powerful and true. I know that we serve a God who, as the prophet Isaiah so beautifully details:

Has come to:

> Comfort All who mourn,
> To provide for those who grieve,
> To bestow a crown of beauty instead of ashes,
> To give the oil of joy instead of mourning,
> And a garment of praise instead of a spirit of despair.
> This he will do so that we may become a planting of the Lord, for the sake of His glory! (Isaiah 61:2-3)

Thank you, Jesus!

The past few months have been a time of deep reflection. I've pored over twenty-five years of journals detailing both joys and difficulties, as well as the countless ways in which God has proven himself faithful in my life.

From the day my 3-year-old self knelt by my bed and prayed a simple prayer, until today, my life has been a steady stream of "Ebenezers"—*thus far hath the Lord helped me*, moments.

I have no reason to doubt that he will continue to lead us, and as Philippians 1:6 declares, "Being confident of this, that he who began a good work in you will carry it on to completion until the day of Jesus Christ."

God gave me a powerful word during our time at home which I put to music just a few weeks ago. It was his mandate to me, and it will be my final word to you, my friends.

> Stand Firm!
> Let nothing shake you!
> God is our defense
> And he will help you.

Stand Firm!
Let nothing move you!
God is our shield;
He will defend you.
Stand Firm!

Stand Firm!
When darkness lingers,
God is our light;
He will deliver.
Stand Firm!
When grief o'ertakes you,
God is our comfort;
He will hold you.
Stand Firm!

Stand Firm!
Though wars are raging,
God is our captain;
He will lead us.
Stand Firm!
When fear surrounds you,
God is our refuge;
He'll protect you.
Stand Firm!

Stand Firm!
Keep on working;
Your labor's not in vain;
The Lord is watching.
Stand Firm!
Keep on praying,
Call upon his name;

The Lord is listening.
Stand Firm!

Stand Firm!
The Lord is coming
To right every wrong
And claim the victory.
Stand Firm!
Don't grow weary;
The battle is the Lord's;
We are victorious.
Stand Firm![17]

17 Kim Collingsworth, *Stand Firm, 2020*

Q & A WITH KIM

While traveling the country singing and playing to nearly 150,000 people each year, our family is often bombarded with questions. Here are a few of the things people seem most curious about:

Why do you travel with your own piano?

The piano is a very integral part of the music we bring to every concert. We didn't start carrying our own concert grand until 2010. In the first ten years of our ministry I survived some disastrous pianos!

One night while playing a rousing rendition of "He Set Me Free" with a track, two black keys flew off the keyboard and into the front row of the audience. An enthusiastic man caught them and stood to his feet, shouting, "I've got them! Who will give me $200 for these?" It was funny but distracting, to say the least.

I remember playing at a high school auditorium in Ohio where there *was* no piano. Phil went into an adjacent gymnasium and found an old blond spinet. I eyed the tired instrument dubiously. The key cover knobs were missing, leaving only dangerous looking screws which jutted out threateningly. I was sure I'd tear my hands to pieces that night and leave a good amount of blood on the keys. It was desperately out of tune, and after playing one number I told Phil, "No more piano!" A man stood up in the audience stating that he had driven two hours that night and wanted to hear me play a certain piece. I acquiesced, but it *was* painful!

And then there was the time when we were late getting into the venue, and we didn't know until the last minute that the piano was tuned a half-step low. I had to transpose all of my piano solos just like that! It wreaked havoc in my mind—for instance, I was playing a "C" but hearing a "B-natural." I was mentally exhausted by the night's end, and I had never worked so hard in my life.

And I will spare you the dreadful details of the night Phil sent me up to play the prelude on a four-octave beginner's electronic keyboard.

When we started receiving calls in the office where people would say, "We're traveling two hours to hear you tonight, and would like to know what kind of piano Kim will be playing on," Phil began to feel the need for me to travel with my own instrument. When God graciously provided for the purchase of "Lucille," I was so grateful. I never asked for a road piano. It may be hard for you to believe, but it was Phil's dream, and he and God made it happen. Hauling a grand piano in and out of concert halls is a lot of work for the crew, but they have a great system of setup and pack up, and from a sound perspective they like knowing what tone and sound to expect each night.

Do you get along?

I like the question because I think it expresses a concern for authenticity.

Perhaps I've addressed this a bit in a previous chapter. I'll just say that we are a very normal...*Christian* family. We have strong opinions and navigate a busy and sometimes stressful life. We spend 150 days and nights together on a bus each year! To say there are never strong "differences of opinion" or causes for irritation would be untruthful.

Very early in the ministry I told the children that we could never expect God's blessing on our ministry if we didn't practice humble love—kindness, respect, patience, and forgiveness. It's our commitment to each other that we don't walk onto the stage with friction between us. When there has been an issue, we clear it up and move on.

Psalm 133:1, 3b states: "How good and pleasant it is when God's people live together in unity!...For there the Lord bestows his blessing, even life forevermore." We desire God's blessing on our family and ministry. Unity pleases the Lord. We are grateful that we truly love each other. And adding two wonderful sons-in-law and a beautiful daughter-in-law to the team has only added to the love and blessing.

Do you all live on the bus all the time?

Believe it or not, there are some who think the bus is our permanent and only dwelling.

The answer is a resounding, *NO!* All the talk in the previous paragraph about love and unity might be out the window if we lived together *all* the time. As much as the CFAM loves travel—and we do—we also love going our separate ways when the bus pulls onto Brannon Road. Even at home, though, I get texts often from various ones asking, "Mom, what are your dinner plans?" Or a FaceTime from Emma, "Nana, can you come and get me?" I love it!

How is it that even your in-law children work in the ministry? Are they really on board?

As our children became young adults and began dating and preparing for marriage, I never for a moment imagined that things would be as they are today. I believe a woman must follow her man, and have told this to our girls very clearly. I know it sounds old-fashioned!

Both our sons-in-law are educated, talented men, and certainly didn't *need* jobs with the CFAM. We were surprised when they both indicated that they *wanted* the girls to keep traveling. The girls *wanted* to keep traveling, too. Our sons-in-law may not have needed us, but God knew that the CFAM needed them. They are both gifted in ways the rest of us are not. I am astounded at what they bring to the table every single day. They are an intricate part of the team. They are technically astute at all the aspects of digital media concepts: filming, editing, livestreaming, and more. They push us to be our very best, and always have a wish list ready to let us know what equipment the CFAM *must* have.

When Phillip was about 10 years old, we stood one night in the green room waiting to sing. I stood watching him, noting that he had grown several inches and felt a twinge of sadness. I said aloud, "Phillip, you are getting so big—soon you'll grow up and leave us."

He said without hesitation, "No, Mom, I'm never going to leave. I'm going to marry someone who will run sound while I sing, and then I'll run sound while she sings." I smiled, and we walked out for the evening concert.

Phillip did grow up and married someone—a beautiful someone who sings—but I don't believe she's ever run sound...yet! We are so grateful for Sharlenae and the blessing she is to Phillip and to the rest of us. And when I have a little more time, I'll tell you about sweet Noah.

Who decides what you wear on stage?

When the children were young, this was an enormous job. I love things to be coordinated nicely, but it took a lot of planning and organization to make it happen. I'd set out with a very small budget and color schemes in mind. When I realized that certain colors are more available than others, depending on what was "in" for the season, it became easier. I did a ton of shopping at Goodwill and other thrift stores. I inherited an ability from my mother to find great deals at discounted prices. The dress I'm wearing on the cover of my *Sunday Morning Ivories II* CD was a steal from the back rack at Goodwill. It had never been worn and was still bearing the tags. What a deal!

Today, the girls and I shop together. We usually have five spring and summer outfits and five fall and winter. Stage clothes never leave the bus, except for cleaning, and I still use lots of coupons and buy from clearance racks. I always love the thrill of a great deal on a beautiful piece of clothing.

We have been asked countless times if we are "legalistic" or if our "church" makes us wear modest clothing. The answer is "no." We have personal convictions about modesty, for which we do not apologize. It is just who we are. I would never want anything that we wear to distract from our mission to share the Gospel through music, but at the same time, we do not judge others who do not hold the same views we do.

How do you stay "fresh" when you are singing the same songs night after night?

First of all, we *haven't* always remained fresh. We've failed and been guilty of operating in the flesh. Those times have usually been prefaced by a season of "too busy." Holding fast to the non-negotiables—days off, corporate worship, meditation on God's Word, prayer, family time—has been paramount to freshness.

We need the body of Christ. We need a church family. Our time at home during this pandemic has highlighted this for us. Watching Emma enjoy Sunday school each week has been a joy. She wouldn't miss it for anything. And when our children were small, I loved watching them go off to Junior Church where I knew teacher Charlotte would reinforce the truths we were instilling in them at home.

A few years ago, we decided as a team to implement another means of grace into our lives. We began a monthly Bible study with a longtime friend and theologian, Dr. Allan Brown. It's a team study. He takes us into the Word, which adds richness and depth to our walk with the Lord. And Dr. Brown isn't afraid to say to us, "How are you doing? Are you living right? God is using you; beware of Satan's schemes." He welcomes questions, and writes our personal prayer requests on 3x5 cards, promising to pray confidentially about each one.

Phil and I received a letter from our son-in-law a few years ago. He expressed he'd been feeling for some time that the CFAM needed to plan and implement team fasts several times each year. We have done so, and this has proved to be an amazing opportunity for spiritual growth and direction, individually and as a team. I'm so grateful that our children are spiritually invested in the ministry.

We are aware of our need. We can't do ministry, nor do we want to do ministry, without the presence and power of God.

Why do you sing while you play piano solos?

I don't really know exactly. I do know that when I arrange a piece of music, the inspiration comes from the lyrics. The ebb and flow of the music is directly related to the "message" of the song. As I play, it's the lyric that inspires me, and I try to communicate it through the keys.

There was a time I feared it was distracting and tried my best to stop! I felt like a bird in a cage, and when Phil told me that my playing sounded a bit reticent or inhibited, I decided to relax and do what came naturally.

What does the set-up for a CFAM concert look like?

In the early days, Phil and a young, eager Phillip did all the set up while the rest of us got ready in a Sunday school room or a nearby hotel. It was rather simple, with minimal equipment.

Things have become a bit more...*complicated*, and today we rely on some amazing people to help make it all happen. Phillip is the production manager and heads up the crew for set-up. Words are inadequate to express our gratefulness for his tireless efforts to make things the absolute best they can be. He never complains, he's very detailed, and is a huge blessing to his dad and me. He lifts the load daily for Phil and takes care of countless 'behind the scenes' details.

We arrive at 10:30-11:00 a.m. for a 7 p.m. concert, usually after driving through the night from the previous venue. We are so thankful for our bus driver, Lowell, Phil's brother-in-law, who drives the bus and gets us to our concert venues in one piece and well-rested.

Phillip, Lowell, Michael, and William unload the trailer with all the sound, media gear, and piano. It takes approximately two and one-half hours to get it all in place.

At around 3 p.m. we have a sound check, which goes for about an hour. Afterward, while we go to an early supper, the pre-scheduled piano tuner arrives to tune Lucille.

From 5:00–6:45 p.m. the bus is a flurry of activity as we all get ready. This has become even more "fun" with grandchildren on the bus. We have survived Emma's toddler years where she frequently helped herself to the girl's toiletries, and we've had some epic cleanups on the bus. Winston is a typical three-year-old boy who loves to throw things. We've had a few mishaps, and have become adept at working around the children *and* the messes they make.

After a two and one-half to three hour concert, we greet people at the product table, and the guys soon get busy reversing the whole setup process!

At around 11:30 p.m. to midnight, the door to the trailer closes, and we all relax for a little while before heading to bed. Some evenings we end up at a Steak 'n Shake or a Sheetz where the crew replaces the energy expended in their twelve-hour day.

And what shall I say about my girls. They are always ready to sing, play, and greet the wonderful folks who come to hear us. Brooklyn, Courtney, and Olivia are a constant source of encouragement to me. They've grown from little girls to smart, capable women who bring so much creativity to the CFAM. And they're generous with wardrobe advice for mom, too! And to their chagrin, I often don't pay attention! They have diverse personalities and interests but if you ask them, they'll all tell you that they love getting on the bus.

I cannot express my gratitude for every person on our team. I shake my head sometimes and wonder how they do what they do. We have been so blessed to have many of our extended family members invested in the CFAM as well. Phil's niece, Danette, runs the office with excellence. Brandon, Phil's nephew, ran our sound for several years and was an integral part of our team. He has gone on to start his own business and is doing *very* well. Of course, we are also blessed with Lowell, and my sister, Vicky, keeps me sane on the home front.

We are thankful for Emily, who travels with us all the time now, is our Social Media Manager, and is a perfect "Mary Poppins" kind of nanny. The kids love her!!